HARDPRESS.NET
HOME OF HARD-TO-FIND BOOKS

The Eternal Filiation of the Son of God Asserted on the Evidence of the Sacred Scriptures
by Frodsham Hodson

Address:
HardPress
8345 NW 66TH ST #2561
MIAMI FL 33166-2626
USA
Email: info@hardpress.net

THE
ETERNAL FILIATION
OF THE
SON OF GOD
ASSERTED

ON THE

EVIDENCE OF THE SACRED SCRIPTURES,

THE

CONSENT OF THE FATHERS OF THE
THREE FIRST CENTURIES,

AND THE

AUTHORITY OF THE NICENE COUNCIL.

BY THE
REV. FRODSHAM HODSON, M. A.
FELLOW OF BRASEN-NOSE COLLEGE, OXFORD.

Ἔστιν ἄρα Ὁ ΛΟΓΟΣ ῾ΥΙΟΣ, ὺκ ΑΡΤΙ γεγονὼς, ἢ ὀνομασθεὶς
῾ΥΙΟΣ, ἀλλ᾽ ΑΕΙ ῾ΥΙΟΣ.
ATHANAS. tom. i. p. 539. Ed. Par. 1698.

OXFORD:
SOLD BY FLETCHER AND HANWELL;
BY F. AND C. RIVINGTON, LONDON; W. LUNN, CAMBRIDGE;
AND T. CRANE, LIVERPOOL.
M DCC XCVI.

MY LORD,

I SHOULD not have prefumed to infcribe the following Tract to your Lordfhip, if you had not, by requefting the publication of it, conferred upon it a value, which can alone entitle it to fo diftinguifhed an honour. Should it in the remoteft degree contribute to the vindication of a doctrine, maintained by the Catholic Church, it would afford me fuch fatisfaction, as I dare hardly anticipate. If it fail of that important end, it will ftill be a confolation to me to have executed a plan, delineated by your Lordfhip, in fuch a manner as to have been honoured by your approbation; and even under the vexation of difappointed hope, I fhall yet rejoice in having had an opportunity, thus gratifying to my feelings, of acknowledging

that

that I am indebted to your Lordfhip's advice for whatever progrefs I have been able to make in the ftudy of Divinity;——an acknowledgment, in which I am perfuaded I fhall be joined by all, who are fortunate enough to be placed within the fphere of your academical authority.

I am, my Lord,

With fentiments of the moft profound refpect,

Your Lordfhip's obliged

and humble fervant,

FRODSHAM HODSON.

LIVERPOOL,
Jan. 16, 1796.

PREFACE.

THE following sheets are the result of an examination into the question, "Whether "the Filiation of the Son of God was ab "Æterno?" — an examination which the Author was directed to undertake, as Probationary Fellow of Brasen-Nose College. For the proofs in favour of the negative side of the question, the Author was referred to the Θεάνθρωπος of Mr. Hawtrey; and whilst he was directed to examine the validity of the arguments there urged by an appeal to the Scriptures, the Fathers, and the Nicene Council; he at the same time was told, with a liberality of mind which disdained to drop any expression that could shackle the freedom of inquiry, to compare, to deliberate, and to determine. Nearly in the same state in which the result of his inquiries was originally submitted to The Right Reverend the Principal of Brasen-Nose, it is now submitted to the public

public. Some few alterations however have been made; some ambitiosa ornamenta, which encumbered the introduction, have been removed, in submission to one, whose judgment always carries with it authority to the Author's mind; and, at the suggestion of the same able critic, one or two corrections have been adopted, which the Author regrets are not more in number, because they are considerable in value.

Should the Author's scriptural view of the question be thought too confined, he is ready to allow, that it might have been expanded with advantage. But, as Mr. Hawtrey's appeal to the Nicene Creed had in some measure made an appeal to the earlier Fathers necessary, he was particularly directed to collect their opinions, as constituting a species of evidence, less accessible to the generality of readers.

He who wishes for more proofs from Scripture may find them in a Sermon " on " the Eternal Generation of the Son of God," by the Bishop of Chester, who, from a comprehensive consideration of the language of the New Testament, has shewn that the idea of an antecedent Filiation is interwoven with the very contexture of Revelation.

As

As the Θεάνθρωπος of Mr. Hawtrey is per-
petually quoted in the courſe of the following examination, it may be proper to apprize
the reader, that it is not the general doctrine
of that valuable work which is here combated ; but only that particular one, which
relates to the Filiation, and which forms, as
it were, an epiſode in the book. For the
reſt, if the voice of an unknown individual
could be heard amidſt the loud applauſes of
the learned, it ſhould be raiſed with the
moſt cordial ſincerity in commendation of
one, who has ſo ably vindicated the Divinity
of our Lord.

Whether the Filiation of the Son of God was

ab Æterno?

No reflecting man can enter into the thorny field of controversy without feelings of reluctance and regret. But, however disheartening may be the prospect, and however arduous the task, a minister of the Gospel is actuated by principles paramount to personal feeling. Even if that satisfaction, with which the mind glows on the discovery of truth in any department of science, were not considered by him as at once an encouragement and a reward to his most active exertions; yet when the object of research is an article of Religion, to the allurements of pleasure are superadded the ties of duty: and, as the sense of so sacred an obligation will operate as an incentive to the undertaking, so, whatever difficulties may occur, He will be animated to persevere by the hopes of that

B   tranquillity

tranquillity of mind, which is the conftant companion of conviction.

> * Αἶψ' ὄγε δυσφρονέων ἐπιλήθεται, ἠδέ τι κηδέων
> Μέμνηται· ταχέως δὲ παρέτραπε δῶρα Θεοῖο.

Much extraneous matter may be excluded, and the labour of inveftigation greatly abridged, by reducing the real object of our refearch to a precife and definite point. With the complicated controverfy then relating to a Trinity in Unity, with which the Chriftian world has been fo long and fo dreadfully convulfed, however intimately our queftion may feem to be connected with it, we have no immediate concern. For the very fubject of our inquiry manifeftly prefuppofes the acknowledged exiftence of fuch Trinity, or at leaft of a fecond Perfon in the Godhead : as it would be prepofterous to inveftigate the relative nature of one, whofe very Being at all was matter of doubtful fpeculation. It is therefore with the avowed Trinitarian that we are at iffue; with him, who allowing the fecond Perfon in the Trinity to have exifted from all eternity in the capacity of the word of God, maintains that * He then only began to be his

---

* Hefiod. Theog. v. 102.

b Θεάνθρωπος τῆς καινῆς Διαθήκης, or, An Appeal to the New Teftament in proof of the Divinity of the Son of God. By Charles Hawtrey, M. A. and Vicar of Bampton, Oxfordfhire. London, 1794. p. 39—43.

Son,

Son, when he became incarnate ; that the Filiation in fhort confifted, and confifted only, in the Incarnation.

Thus, it has lately been afferted [c] " that " the Eternal Generation of the Son of God is " not to be fupported by any thing in the " New Teftament." It may with more truth be replied that the doctrine, which teaches that the Filiation commenced at the Incarnation, can not boaft of any fcriptural proof, but what arifes from a conjectural Interpretation, which may perhaps be fhewn to be unfounded ; and from an attempt to eftablifh a diftinction, which was probably never intended. Still, whatever be our fuccefs in combating this new hypothefis, if the Eternal Filiation cannot be proved by the holy Scriptures, he, who fubfcribes to the Articles of Religion, muft, in conformity with the fixth of them, abandon it as a neceffary article of Faith. And yet after having been habituated to the Liturgy of our National Church, he will certainly feel fome ftrong prepoffeffions in its favour, and fome compunction at parting with it. Accuftomed in the Te Deum, which he believes to have been compofed at leaft as early [d] as in the

[c] Id. p. 43. 185. 187.
[d] Bingham's Origines Ecclefiafticæ, l. xiv. c. 2. p. 400. vol. 6.

beginning

beginning of the fixth century, to addrefs Chrift as " the everlafting Son of the ever-" lafting Father;" in the Litany to fuppli-cate God, the Father, and God, the Son; in the Confeffion of our Chriftian Faith, commonly called, the Creed of St. Athana-fius, to profefs a belief that the Son is un-create and eternal; and in the Nicene Creed to acknowledge the Son, as " begotten by " his Father before all ages," and the Holy Ghoft as " proceeding from the Father and " the Son;"---accuftomed to thefe profeffions of faith, and familiarized to the leffer Doxo-logy, all fanctioned by the authority of the Church, he muft be excufed if he ftill fuf-pects that the Doctrine maintained in them refts on a broader and a firmer foundation than the precarious bafis of human Invention. Recollecting too that there is [e] another of our Articles of Religion, which holds that our " three Creeds may be proved by moft cer-" tain warrants of holy Scripture;" he will doubtlefs paufe awhile, before he withdraws his belief from a Doctrine, thus declared, by the pious compilers of our Liturgy and Arti-cles, to be the doctrine of Infpiration. In the commencement therefore of the invefti-

[e] The 8th.

gation,

gation, he cannot perhaps wholly divest himfelf of prejudice; but yet he will not think
that the "quicquid in religione vetus reti-
"nendum eft," is to be fo pertinacioufly ad-
hered to, as to preclude the extirpation of
Herefy, however venerable for its Antiquity,
and however endeared to us by early Prejudice.

To produce, even under the aufpices of
ancient Commentators, proofs which are liable to general objections, might be thought
to argue a diftruft in the fufficiency of our
Evidence without them. I fhall therefore
pafs over the affiftance to be derived from
the Old Teftament; as the ftrongeft paffages,
thofe I mean which occur in the Pfalms,
may, as well as thofe which occur in the
Prophets, be thought defcriptive of what the
Meffiah was to be at his advent, rather than
declaratory of what he was before.

Betwixt, however, a general indifpofition to
admit evidence of a certain ftamp, and a difference of opinion with regard to the meaning of a particular word, a diftinction muft
be allowed; fo that though we decline introducing the one, we fhall not be inconfiftent,
if we combat the other.

Thus, we would appeal to the words, ᶠ πρω-

ᶠ Coloff. i. 15.

τότοκος

τότοκος πάσης κτίσεως, by which St. Paul defcribes the Son of God, as likely to decide
the queftion, though Commentators have
doubted, whether they imply priority or preeminence of birth. For reafons which we
will affign, their tranflation feems to be the
beft, who render the words, " born before
" every creature ;" thus decompounding πρω-
7ότοκος, and in the conftruction transferring πρὸ
to πάσης κτίσεως. Nor is this a fingular inftance of a facred Writer, giving the force of
the comparative degree to πρῶτος. [ᵍ] Schmidius adduces feveral examples from profane
authors as well as from the New Teftament, of πρῶτος, and words compounded of
πρῶτος, having this comparative fignification.
Other, and very appofite inftances may be
found in [ʰ] Mr. Stephens's fermon, on " The
" Divine Perfons one God by an unity of
" nature :" or, " that our Saviour is one
" God with his Father, by an Eternal Gene-
" ration from his fubftance." Mr. Hawtrey
of courfe, in order to be confiftent, and pre-
ferve his hypothefis from immediate refutation, rejects this interpretation, but is rather
fparing of argument to corroborate his own.
When a new tranflation is to fuperfede a re-

[ᵍ] Schmidius in Luc. c. ii. ver. 2.
[ʰ] Preached before the Univerfity of Oxford, 1722.

ceived

ceived one in order to determine a doctrinal controverſy, it ought to come recommended to us by the ſupport of biblical criticiſm : but no argument, either founded on its peculiar agreement with the context, or the ſimilar uſe of it in other paſſages is brought forward ; unleſs indeed we ought to except the ' aſking of a queſtion, which the ancient Commentators will ſufficiently anſwer ; and the quotation of a ᵏ verſe in which πρωτότοκος occurs, where however the Author himſelf confeſſes that it is uſed in the ſenſe of firſtborn. Perhaps the confirmation to be derived from biblical criticiſm was withheld, becauſe it might be found detailed in thoſe Annotators, with whom Mr. Hawtrey coincides. It is true; his interpretation of preeminent is defended both by orthodox and heterodox, by thoſe who affirm and thoſe who deny the Eternity of the Son ; ˡ by Grotius and Hammond, by Wetſtein and Locke. But might not the two firſt incline to it from an apprehenſion, that if they rendered it " firſt-born " of every creature," it might be perverted

---

ᶦ " If πρωτότοκος ſignifies priority in point of time or exiſt-" ence, will it not be to blend Jeſus Chriſt with the maſs of " the creation, to make him thereby the firſt created of the " works of God ?" p. 185.
ᵏ Coloſſ. i. 17.
ˡ The three firſt in their notes on Coloſſ. i. 15. and the laſt tranſlates πρωτότοκον, chief, Rom. viii. 29.

into

into a confeffion of the Son's being a creature ? and might not the latter adopt it, becaufe to have tranflated it firft-born would
have been an unequivocal acknowledgment
of the Son's Eternity ? To the authority of
the names, however, juft recited, we can
oppofe others equally great and authori-
tative ; Cafaubon and Bengelius, Beza and
Erafmus. Of thofe other critics who agree
in the interpretation, " genitus ante omnem
" creaturam," Schmidius ought not to be
omitted, as being every way qualified, from
his accurate knowledge of the other paffages,
in which the word is ufed, to decide upon its
meaning ; nor [m] Luther, as giving us the
fentiments of one who with fuch extraordinary ability promoted the Reformation. The
Vulgate too, and the Latin tranflations of the
Ethiopic and Arabic verfions render πρωτότοκος, primogenitus ; as again the Syriac ufes
the fynonymous word, primigenius, which
Gefner explains by primitivus. [n] Tertullian
too explains primogenitus, " ante omnia geni-
" tus ;" whilft of the more ancient Commentators, it ought to be obferved that [o] Theo-

---

[m] " Der erftgeborne von allen creaturen." Luther.
[n] Tertullian adverfus Prax. p. 503. Ed. Par.
[o] Theodoret's comment on the paffage is, ὡς πρὸ πάσης κτίσεως γεννηθείς. Tom. iii. p. 346. Ed. Sirmond.

doret

doret and [b] Theophylact support our tranflation.—I forbear to quote others, as the con-
fenfus veterum may be feen by confulting
Suicer on the word.

I cannot but be aware, that the difference
of opinion with regard to πρωτότοκος, which,
it may be faid, prevails amongft men, alike
diftinguifhed for their critical attainments,
will, in the prefent ftage of our Inquiry,
hardly juftify me in arguing from it. Added
to this, the coincidence on this point, which
we have acknowledged, between men of directly oppofite habits of thinking on other
the moft effential topics, may poffibly create
a prepoffeffion in favour of the fenfe we
wifh to exclude. But a little reflection will
greatly weaken the force of the objection
built upon that difference in one cafe, and
that coincidence of fentiment in the other.

The Advocates of the Socinian fcheme, it
muft be remembered, are not competent
Judges. They come to the examination with
a ftrong and ftubborn prejudice ingrafted on
their minds, from which we may à priori in-
fer their decifion. For if they were to allow
the tranflation, "born before every creature,"

---

[b] Theophylact's words are, βούλεται δεῖξαι, ὅτι πρὸ πάσης κτίσεώς ἐστι ὁ Τίός· πῶς ὤν; διὰ γεννήσεως. p. 635. In Pauli Epift.
comment. Ed. Lindfel, Epifc. Heref.

the

the conceffion would be a plain acknowledgment of the palpable falfehood of their creed. Nor let the charge of prejudice, with the view of impeaching our interpretation, be retorted againft us ; for, as we have other and ftronger proofs to refort to in order to fubftantiate our faith, our decifion, as indeed is proved by the examples of Grotius and Hammond, is not of neceffity fuch as may be anticipated from our preconceived notions of Chrift. On the contrary, it may fairly be prefumed, what his judgment will be, who by the admiffion of a particular fignification would falfify his religious tenets and at once plead guilty to the charge of herefy.

Again ; the Athanafians, who interpret it of Dignity or Regeneration, were probably deterred from perfifting in the tranflation, " firft-born of every creature," by the unfair advantage which the deniers of our Lord's Divinity would have taken of fuch tranflation. Confcious that the doctrine, which they themfelves maintained, wanted not the affiftance of this tranflation, they did not think the fupport to be derived from it equivalent to the hazard of affording Socinianifm any hold to faften on.

But, poffibly, greater deference may be paid to thofe, who in the character of Philologifts

logifts merely give us the meaning of the
word; as their judgments may be fuppofed
to be unclouded by the mift of theological
prejudice. Here then, we find Suidas and
Hefychius agree in defining it, ὁ πρῶτος τεχ-
θείς; a definition, which, it is not neceffary
to add, the etymon of the word confirms.

Let us in the laft place inquire, what fignification the word has in the general ufage
of the writers of the New Teftament; the
fafeft mode perhaps of developing obfcure, or
defining doubtful expreffions. ⁹ Peirce, in his
elaborate Commentary on the Epiftle to the
Coloffians, fays, that "the word πρωτότοκος is
" never ufed, in the New Teftament, in any
" other fenfe than firft-born." Without ftop-
ping to analyze every paffage in which it occurs, it may be fufficient to obferve that the
facred writers are often guilty of the groffeft
tautology, if it is to be tranflated, preeminent; and to advert to one inftance, which,
if it fhould be deemed an exception to Mr.
Peirce's remark, muft I think be allowed to
be the only one; and to another, where by
confulting the word in the Old Teftament to
which it refers, and for which indeed it is
fubftituted, we may determine the fenfe with

⁹ Paraphrafe and Notes on the Epift. of St. Paul, p. 12.

accuracy.

accuracy. [r] In one paſſage in the Epiſtle to the Hebrews, we find πρωτοτόκων; and the tranſlation, which ſeems beſt to ſuit the exigency of the place, is not the firſt-born, but they who were to enjoy the privilege of the firſt-born; i. e. who were to inherit the birth-right of everlaſting life, covenanted to them by the Goſpel. [s] In another paſſage of this ſame Epiſtle, we find πρωτότοκια uſed, as a correſpondent term for בכור, as it occurs in the Book of [t] Exodus. Now בכור ſignifies " firſt-born" as often as it is found in the Pentateuch, and indeed every where elſe in the Old Teſtament, except in the inſtances which are mentioned by Taylor. That it here does not come under his firſt exception is more than probable, as אלה may be underſtood of the great ones, and is indeed rendered Princes in the margin of our Engliſh Bible; and that it cannot come under the latter is clear, as they could not be ſaid to be highly favoured by God, who were deſtroyed by him. So that here, as indeed throughout the whole of the New Teſtament, the word muſt be underſtood of firſt-born: whilſt, on the other hand, no inſtance can be adduced of its ſignifying preeminent; for even,

[r] c. xii. v. 23.　　　　　[s] c. xi. v. 28.
[t] Exod. c. xii. v. 12.

if

if in chap. xii. v. 23. of the Epiſtle to the Hebrews already noticed, there ſhall be thought to be a deviation from its primary and general ſignification, it muſt at the ſame time be acknowledged that it conveys no idea of preeminence. He then, who fairly balances the weight of evidence in favour of the two interpretations; who places in one ſcale the authority of the ancient Verſions, Commentators and Lexicographers, together with the preſumptive proof ariſing from the uniform ſenſe in which the word is uſed in the other paſſages of the New Teſtament; and in the other, the ſuſpicious authority of thoſe Annotators, who ſupport the other tranſlation, with a due allowance for the force of their teſtimony being abated by the circumſtances to which we adverted above; he, who thus weighs the comparative evidence, cannot, I think, but confeſs that the proofs of the former preponderate.

So much for the external evidence; and with regard to the internal, that this interpretation is well adapted to the context, will be plain from obſerving the other terms which the Apoſtle uſes, and the probable ſcope of his reaſoning[a]. "Giving thanks,"

[a] Coloſſ. c. i. ver. 12—16.

ſays

says he, " to the Father — who hath tranf-
" lated us into the kingdom of his dear Son
" —who is the *Image* of the invifible God,
" born before every creature." And how is
this proved ? " *Becaufe*," fays St. Paul, " all
" things were created by *him* ;" whence it
neceffarily follows that he muft, in our fenfe
of the words, have been πρωτότοκος πάσης κλί-
σεως. With Origen we may afk, πῶς ἐκ ἔδα
αὐτὸν εἶναι πρὸ αὐτῶν, καὶ ἐν ἀρχῇ, τῆς ὑπάρξεως
αὐτῶν κτίσην ὄντα ;

Should this attempt to afcertain the real
meaning of St. Paul be thought to have en-
groffed too much attention, it furely will not
be deemed in tenui labor, when it is remembered that the admiffion of the truth of
our Interpretation involves in it the down-
fall of Mr. Hawtrey's hypothefis. And yet,
after all, to have endeavoured with fuch mi-
nutenefs to eftablifh the propriety of tranf-
lating " born before every creature," may be
thought an unneceffary though not an ufelefs
employment ; for in whatever fenfe thefe
words be underftood, the paffage ftill furnifhes us with an irrefragable proof of the
Son's exiftence before the creation of the
world. For to what antecedent does the pro-
noun αὐτῷ, in the 16th verfe, refer? Clearly
to υἱῷ in the 13th; and as the Apoftle's affertion

tion is that " all things were created by the
" *Son*," it can require no reafoning to fhew
that the *Son* muft have exifted before. To
whichever tranflation therefore of πρωτότοκος
πάσης κτίσεως the preference be given, this
magnificent paffage ftill fupplies a direct and
fubftantial proof of the *Son*'s previous exiftence.

A fimilar argument might be drawn from
the [x] Epiftle to the Hebrews, where the *Son*
is again reprefented as the author of the
creation. But we fhall not be content with
merely deducing from the creative power
afcribed to the Son, the neceffity of his prior
exiftence ; as the comparifon of this paffage
and the one quoted from the Epiftle to the
Coloffians with [y] St. John's Gofpel will go
at once to the total fubverfion of the imagi-
nary diftinction between the Word and the
Son. St. John fays, " all things were made
" by the *Word* ;" St. Paul as before cited,
and the author of the Epiftle to the Hebrews fay, " by the *Son*, God made the
" worlds." Either, then, one of them is
wrong,---a fuppofition not compatible with
the plenary infpiration attributed to the facred
writers ; or, if they are both right, the Word

[x] c. i. v. 2.   [y] c. i. v. 3.

and

and the Son mean one and the fame preexift-
ing power. If the Epiftle to the Hebrews
be adjudged to St. Paul, we find the fame
implied affertion of the Son's prior exiftence
repeated by one, who, from the different
vifions which were vouchfafed to him, was
likely, as far as it was poffible, to have pene-
trated into the moft myfterious nature of the
Godhead : if it be not, our argument is
equally conclufive ; as we fhall then have
the doctrine of one infpired writer confirmed
by the teftimony of another. So that at all
events, we are reduced to the dilemma either
of branding the Evangelift or the Apoftle
with the guilt of falfehood, or of acknowledging the eternal identity of the Word and
the Son. As they who believe that both the
Gofpel and the Epiftle were compofed under
the fuperintending influence of the Holy
Ghoft cannot admit the very poffibility of
the former, they will of courfe acquiefce in
the latter alternative.

But further ; he, who is at all converfant
with the writings of the Fathers cannot but
have obferved the indifcriminate ufe which
they make of the terms Λόγος and Υἱός ; af-
cribing indifferently to the Perfon, charac-
terized by each of thofe titles, the work of
creation. That they thought themfelves juf-
tified

tified in this promiscuous use of the words is clear, because they maintained the personal Identity of the Word and the Son. For the present, one or two instances of this mode of writing may be sufficient; as I shall have occasion to be more copious in such examples, both when animadverting on the very passage on which Mr. Hawtrey's distinction rests, and when adducing the opinion of the primitive Christians.

The following extract from Justin Martyr will shew that He at least thought the Word and the Son synonymous [z]. " But I will give " you another proof also," says he, " from " the Scriptures, that God in the beginning " before all creatures *generated* from himself " a certain rational power, which is called " by the Holy Ghost the Lord's Glory, and " sometimes *Son* — and sometimes *Word*." Tatian [a] calls the *Word*, " the *first-begotten* " work of the Father ;" and Irenæus [b] grounds his refutation of the Valentinian Heresy on

---

[z] Μαρτύριον δὲ καὶ ἄλλο ὑμῖν ἀπὸ τῶν γραφῶν δώσω, ὅτι ἀρχὴν πρὸ πάντων τῶν κτισμάτων ὁ Θεὸς ΓΕΓΕΝΝΗΚΕ δύναμίν τινα ἐξ ἑαυτοῦ λογικὴν, ἥτις καὶ δόξα Κυρίου ὑπὸ τοῦ πνεύματος τοῦ ἁγίου καλεῖται, ποτὲ δὲ ΥΙΟΣ,—καὶ ΛΟΓΟΣ. Dial. cum Tryph. Jud.

[a] Ὁ δὲ λόγος ἔργον ΠΡΩΤΟΤΟΚΟΝ (τοῦ πνεύματος, var. lect.) τοῦ πατρός. p. 21. Ed. Worth.

[b] ΕΝΟΣ καὶ ΤΟΥ ΑΥΤΟΥ δεικνυμένου ΛΟΓΟΥ — καὶ ΥΙΟΥ Θεοῦ, καὶ ΤΟΥΤΟΥ ΑΥΤΟΥ σαρκωθέντος ὑπὲρ ἡμῶν. λέλυται ἡ τῆς Ὀγδοάδος σκηνοπηγία. Iren. l. i. c. 20. p. 42. Ed. Grabe.

C

the

the demonſtrated Identity of the Word and the Son.

But Mr. Hawtrey perhaps, anxious to evade the preſſure of evidence thus hoſtile to his ſyſtem, and to reſcue from a fate ſo untimely a Doctrine which is expected to remove all the difficulties which impede a general confeſſion of Chriſt's Divinity, may ſuggeſt ſome ſubterfuge. He may ſay perhaps, that the Apoſtles and Fathers uſed the terms thus promiſcuouſly, becauſe He, who was originally λόγος, afterwards became υἱὸς, and continued to be ſo, at the time they wrote. But ſurely to deſcribe him as acting in the character of υἱὸς at a period, before he had aſſumed that Character is an inaccuracy, which they, who ſcruple not to impute it to the Fathers, would ſhrink from the imputation of themſelves. Would an Hiſtorian of the reign of Charles the Firſt, in deſcribing the battle of Naſeby, ſay that the King's troops were defeated by the *Protector's?* Or if he did, would he not be cenſured for an Anachroniſm in language? And if human wiſdom conſiders ſuch an anticipation of a future title an errour amounting to falſehood, we may ſurely give the Apoſtle and the Fathers credit for equal Sagacity. But be this as it may, the learned author of Θεάνθρωπος muſt

muſt be cautious how he ſanctions a lati-
tude of interpretation, which may be turned
againſt himſelf, or urges a plea, which, if admitted, will conſiderably weaken, if not
wholly deſtroy, the force of that *appropriate*
application of the terms λόγος and υἱὸς, which
he conceives St. John to make, in the opening of his Goſpel. For if, as he ſuppoſes, the
Evangeliſt intended by a diſtinction of title
to mark a diſtinction of character, the Queſtion naturally occurs, how happens it, that
his *followers*, nay his *contemporaries* ſhould
pay ſuch little reſpect to the momentous preciſion of the beloved diſciple of their Lord,
as to apply to him, I had almoſt ſaid with
undiſtinguiſhing blindneſs, (and the language
would not be too ſtrong on Mr. Hawtrey's
hypotheſis) a title *before* his Incarnation,
which he had not till *after* it ? Are we to
ſay that St. John's penetrating mind pierced
into the hidden myſteries of God, and deve-
loped that doctrine, which Mr. Hawtrey
imagines he inculcates; but that the doctrine
of St. Paul and the Fathers is the blundering
invention of half informed Novitiates ? Or
are we to believe that they all meant to
teach the ſame doctrine, but that the words
of St. John are the elaborate language of
preciſion and deſign, whilſt thoſe of the

C 2   others

others are the vague and carelefs terms of in-
difference or chance? No! The fair and obvious inference is, that the Apoftle and the
Fathers confidered the two terms as expreffive of the *fame Relation* to God; they thought,
that, as the λόγος is an *emanation* or *progeny*
of the heavenly Mind, it might be ufed as
metaphorically fignificant of the fame relative
connexion of the Second Perfon with the
Firft which is conveyed by υἱὸς; an expreffion,
which gives us an idea of connected exiftence
not equally remote from vulgar apprehenfion.

But as this reafoning affects the data, on
which Mr. Hawtrey builds his fyftem, it
may feem premature, if we do not examine
them more minutely. We will therefore in
the firft inftance proceed to the difcuffion of
the fact, (for a fact it certainly is) which is
the main ftay of his conjecture.

St. John, fpeaking of our Saviour in his
pre-exifting ftate, calls him λόγος; but after
his Incarnation, he drops the appellation λόγος, and calls him υἱός. Now in this change
of title our Author difcovers a change of character; in which he has, I believe, the me-
rit of " qui primus invenit," in the ftricteft
fenfe of Bentley's limitation [c]. None of the

* Pref. to the Differtation on Phalaris, p. 94.

ancient

ancient [4] Commentators at leaſt can conteſt
the praiſe of Originality with him, as will be
ſeen from their ſhort-ſighted ſtrictures on
this Chapter.

Thus Baſil [*], in his Homily on the words
" In the beginning was the Word," ſays,
" St. John diſcourſing concerning the *only-*
" *begotten* has called him λόγος.—For what
" reaſon does he call him λόγος ? That it
" might be ſhewn, that he came forth from
" the Mind. Why λόγος? Becauſe he was *be-*
" *gotten* without the intervention of paſſion.
" Why λόγος ? Becauſe he is the *image* of
" him who begot him, exhibiting in himſelf
" him who begot him, whole and entire."
Again ; " he has therefore called him λόγος,
" in order that he might place before you
" the *Generation* void of paſſion on the part
" of the Father, and might teach you the
" perfect exiſtence of the Son, and by theſe

---

[4] I ſpeak only of the commentators on this verſe ; for there
is one paſſage, if not two, in Hippolytus, which will be conſidered hereafter, which may be thought in ſome degree to rob
Mr. Hawtrey of the praiſe of original Invention.

[*] Περὶ τῦ ΜΟΝΟΓΕΝΟΥΣ διαλιγόμινός σοι, ΛΟΓΟΝ ἶπιν. — Διὰ
τί λόγος ; ἶια διιχθῆ ὅτι ἰκ τῦ νῦ σροῆλθι. Διὰ τί λόγος : ὅτι ἀπαθῶς
'ΕΓΕΝΝΗΘΗ· διὰ τί λόγος ; ὅτι εἰκὼν τῦ ΓΕΝΝΗΣΑΝΤΟΣ, ὅλοι ἰν
ἰαυτῷ δεικνὺς τὸν ΓΕΝΝΗΣΑΝΤΑ.
ΛΟΓΟΝ ἶι ἶπιν, ἶια τὴν ἀπαθῆ (var. lect. ἀληθῆ) σοι ΓΕΝΝΗ-
ΣΙΝ τῦ ΠΑΤΡΟΣ παραστήσῃ, καὶ τὴν τιλιίαν ὕπαρξίν σοι θιαλογήσῃ,
καὶ τὴν 'ΑΧΡΟΝΟΝ ΣΥΝΑΦΕΙΑΝ τῦ 'ΥΙΟΥ πρὸς πατίρα διὰ τύτων
ἰνδιίξηται. Homil. xvi. tom. i. p. 435. Ed. Par.

" means

" means demonſtrate the *eternal* connexion
" of the *Son* with the Father." Preciſely to
the ſame effect is the general ſcope of his
reaſoning throughout the whole of his ſecond Book againſt Eunomius.

That Chryſoſtom ᶠ conſidered the Word in
this paſſage as ſynonymous with the Son appears from the Queſtion which he aſks in his
homily on this verſe. " Why does St. John,
" having omitted the Father, ſpeak of the
" *Son ?* Becauſe the former was manifeſt to
" all, if not as Father, yet as God ; but the
" *only-begotten* was not known." It is unne-
ceſſary to multiply quotations from him, as
the ſame idea pervades his whole commentary.

Cyril ᵍ Archbiſhop of Alexandria under-
takes from theſe words of St. John to prove
" that the *only-begotten* is eternal ;" and ſoon
after aſſerts that " as the *Son* is older than
" the ages or worlds themſelves, he could
" not have been *begotten* within the limits of
" time."

ᶠ Τί δήποτ' ἂν τὸν πατέρα ἀφεὶς περὶ τῦ 'ΥΙΟΥ διαλέγεται ; ὅτι
ἐκεῖνος μὲν δῆλος ἅπασιν ἦν, εἰ δὲ μὴ ὡς πατὴρ, ἀλλ' ὡς Θεός· ὁ δὲ
ΜΟΝΟΓΕΝΗΣ ἠγνοεῖτο. Chryſoſt. in c. i. Johan. Homil. p. 15.
Ed. Front. Ducæe.

ᵍ Ὅτι ἀΐδιος, καὶ πρὸ τῶν αἰώνων 'Ο ΜΟΝΟΓΕΝΗΣ. Comment.
in Johan. tom. iv. p. 9. Ed. Aubert. Par.
'Επειδήπερ καὶ αὐτῶν ἐςι τῶν αἰώνων πρεσβύτερος 'Ο 'ΥΙΟΣ, τὸ μὲν
ΕΝ ΧΡΟΝΩ ΓΕΓΕΝΝΗΣΘΑΙ διαφεύξεται. p. 11.

Origen

Origen [b] on the paffage tells us that by the Word St. John meant the Son ; and Theophylact [1] to the Queftion why the Evangelift did not fay, in the beginning was the Son, gives an anfwer analogous to that of Bafil ; and adds that the paffage proves that the *Son* was *co-eternal* with the Father. That Irenæus [k] underftood St. John in this fenfe is plain from almoft every page ; and in one place he directly accufes thofe of diftorting the Scriptures, who make λόγος one perfon, and μονογενὴς another.

To the Commentators already adduced, others might be added, who are omitted as being in point of antiquity and general efteem of lefs weight than thofe we have felected ; but whofe interpretations may be found detailed in the Catena Græcorum Patrum in fanctum Johannem [1].

Thofe Fathers then, it fhould feem, who allude to the two titles λόγος and υἱὸς, clearly confidered them as fynonyms ; and the moft

---

[b] Λόγον πῶς τὸν υἱὸν, κ. τ. λ. Orig. tom. ii. p. 17. Ed. Huet.

[1] Ἵνα μὴ—ποήσωμεν γίνωσιν ἐμπαθῆ καὶ σωματικὴν, τότε ἵνεκεν λόγον αὐτὸν ἐκάλεσιν· ἵνα σὺ μάθῃς ὅτι ὥσπερ ὁ λόγος ΓΕΝΝΑΤΑΙ ἐκ τῶ νοὸς ἀπαθῶς, ᾗ ἄλλως δὲ κ. τ. λ. and σαφέστερον δείκνυσι ΣΥΝΑΙΔΙΟΝ τὸν ὙΙΟΝ τῷ πατρί· κ. τ. λ. Theoph. in quatuor Evang. p. 555—556. Ed. Par.

[k] Παρατρέποντες κ. τ. λ. p. 41. l. 38. Ed. Grabe.

[1] Ed. Balthaf. Corder. e foc. Jef. Antwerp. 1630.

ancient

ancient Commentators on the paſſage ob-
ſerved, as we have ſeen, the change of appel-
lations, but accounted for it upon a very different principle; upon a principle juſt and
obvious, the application of which will not
indeed, like Mr. Hawtrey's conjecture, ſhew
that Hereſy has contaminated the Catholic
Faith for ſeventeen centuries; but which is
yet at once adapted to the exigentia loci, and
countenanced by the higheſt authority of Antiquity. So that from that very appellation,
which in the opinion of the primitive Chriſtians was adopted as the ſureſt precaution
againſt any miſconceptions of the tranſcen-
dent nature of Chriſt's Eternal Generation,
the author of Θεάνθρωπος would extract a proof
of his Filiation being temporal, and the re-
ſult of his Incarnation !

- As the conſent of Antiquity proves that
the Evangeliſt's object in uſing λόγος, was to
expreſs a Generation of a high and peculiar
kind; ſo perhaps alſo he might be induced
to introduce *both* terms into his Goſpel, from
a wiſh to inculcate in limine, in oppoſition
to thoſe philoſophizing Chriſtians who taught
that λόγος was the offspring of μονογενὴς, the
Identity of him who was indifferently called
by both titles. But whatever was his motive
for beginning with λόγος, a probable reaſon
at

at leaſt may be aſſigned for the ſubſtitution of. υἱὸς, without having recourſe to the ſuppo-ſition that he changed his terms, in conſe-quence of a change in the nature of the Per-ſon. ſpoken of. For if St. John had perſe-vered in the uſe of λόγος, and had ſaid, we beheld his Glory as the Glory of the only be-gotten *Word* of God, he would not have conveyed to exoteric ears any determinate Idea ; for the mind, being ſtored with no previous notion of the appearance of ſuch Word, with which to compare the Glory that was beheld, could not recognize the ſi-milarity. ·   ·

Is it not then very probable that St. John changed his language in accommodation to the unenlightened mind ; and meant not, by the " Glory of the only-begotten Son," to inſinuate any newly acquired Glory ? Our bleſſed Lord himſelf ſeems to imply, in his earneſt prayer to the Father, that he had from all eternity the glory of a *Son*. For why ſhould he ſay, " O *Father*, glorify thou " me with thine own ſelf, with the Glory " which I had with thee (the Father) before " the world was ᵐ," if he had not alſo, before the world was, exiſted in the glorious capa-

---

ᵐ John c. xvii. v. 5.

city

city of the *Son* of God ? What favours the inference which I would draw from thefe words is, that this very text is quoted by Cyprian [a] in proof of his pofition, " Chriftum " *primogenitum* effe, et ipfum effe fapientiam, " per quem omnia facta fint." But Mr. Hawtrey feems to forget, that, though St. John might actually mean that they " *beheld* " his Glory as the Glory of the only-begotten " Son of God" in confequence of his Incarnation, it yet by no means follows that he had not that filial Glory before. The Son, it muft be recollected, in his unembodied ftate is not vifible to mortal eye ; and therefore to affert that in confequence of his Incarnation they " beheld his Glory as the Glory of the " only-begotten Son of God," is perfectly re-concileable with his prior though invifible exiftence in that character. In fhort, the Incarnation might be the commencement of the *corporeal manifeftation* of that Glory, without being the origin of the Glory itfelf ; and the whole may be accurately paraphrafed by a paffage from St. Barnabas. Τότε ΕΦΑΝΕ-ΡΩΣΕΝ ἑαυτὸν υἱὸν Θεῦ εἶναι. Εἰ γὰρ μὴ ἦλθεν ἐν σαρκὶ, πῶς ἂν ἐσώθημεν ἄνθρωποι, ΒΛΕΠΟΝ-ΤΕΣ αὐτόν; ὅτι τὸν μέλλοντα μὴ εἶναι ἥλιον——

---

[a] Cyprian. p. 31. Ed. Ox. 1682.

βλέποντες,

βλέποντες, ἐκ ἰσχύυσιν εἰς ἀκτῖνας αὐτῦ ἀντοφ-
θαλμῆσαι [•].

There are paſſages in St. John's Epiſtles
which by implication at leaſt militate againſt
that diſtinction of character, which Mr. Hawtrey diſcovers in the opening of his Goſpel:
thoſe I mean, where he endeavours to move
our ſenſibility and awaken our gratitude, by
reminding us of the Love of God, who " ſent
" his only-begotten Son into the world, that
" we might live through bim [•]." Now in
the firſt place, if it had been the Word, and
not the Son who came in the fleſh, St. John in
ſtrictneſs of language would have ſaid, " God
" ſent his Word," as the Perſon ſent, according to Mr. Hawtrey, was not Son, till after
his aſſumption of human nature; ſo that
this mode of expreſſion ſeems, I think, to
argue an antecedent exiſtence of the *Son*.
The Context ſtrengthens this opinion; for St.
John there labours to excite in us gratitude
to God and charity to Man, by calling to
our recollection *parental* feelings; language,
which is not ſo peculiarly appropriate, unleſs
the Eternal Filiation be admitted. " [•] Herein
" is Love, not that we loved God, but that
" he loved us, and ſent his Son to be the

* Barnab. Epiſt. c. v. p. 16. Ed. Cotel.
P 1 John c. iv. v. 9.
º 1 John c. iv. v. 10, 11. Compare John c. iii. v. 16.

" propitiation

" propitiation for our fins. Beloved, if God
" *fo* loved us, we ought alfo to love one ano-
" ther." I am far from meaning to infinuate,
that if Mr. Hawtrey's notion of the nature
of Chrift be received, the mercy of the Almighty, as exhibited in Man's Redemption,
is not ftill immeafurably great ; or fuch, as
that arguments may not be derived from it
irrefiftibly powerful to overwhelm the hardeft
heart ; to make our piety to God more ar-
dent, and our charity to man more exten-
five. But furely, though we ftill acknowledge that appeal to our gratitude to be for-
cible which is founded on the Love difplayed
by God in accepting the vicarious facrifice of
his Son, it yet lofes fomewhat of its energy
from the idea of Chrift being that Son only
in an adfcititious fenfe ; whilft on the other
hand we feel heightened that tendernefs of
fentiment, mingled with religious awe, which
involuntarily fprings up in the mind, when
we contemplate the Everlafting Son leaving
the bofom of his Everlafting Father, to become a facrificial Atonement for fin. In confirmation of this reafoning let me add, our
Saviour's own affecting words, " Father, thou
" *lovedft* me before the foundation of the
" world ' ;"—a declaration this of *paternal*

* John xvii. v. 24.

affection

affection on the one part, which feems to imply on the other, the exiftence of a *Son* as the object of it.

There are too, it may be remarked, fome texts in which our Saviour fays, that no one knows who the Father is but the Son, and who the Son is but the Father[*] : and there is one, in which he afferts their commenfurate knowledge of each other ; " as the Fa-" ther knoweth me, even fo know I the Fa-" ther[']." Now with regard to the firft, they exclude the Word (except whilft the difpenfation of Θεάνθρωπος continues, for after the termination of it he is a diftinct Perfon) from participating in that knowledge, which yet, on Mr. Hawtrey's hypothefis, he muft have had long before the *Son* exifted. And with regard to the latter, as on this fame hypothefis, the Son, as *Son*, could only have known the Father from the time of his union with the λόγος, but the Father, as being omnifcient, muft from all eternity have known who and what the Son would be : under thefe circumftances I fay, would our Saviour have declared that the Son's knowledge of the Father was commenfurate with the Father's knowledge of the Son ? Or

[*] Matt. c. xi. v. 27.   Luke c. x. v. 22.
['] John c. x. v. 15.

again,

again, would he, nay I may fay, with reverence be it fpoken, could He, confiftently
with the fimplicity of Truth, have afferted
fuch an abfolute unity of *Father* and *Son*, as
he often does ", if the exiftence of the one
had been pofterior to the exiftence of the
other ? Again ; as the Father cannot be denied to be eternal ; if the *Son* were not fo
too, could he have faid, " *as* the Father hath
" life in himfelf, *fo* hath he given to the Son
" to have life in himfelf *?" Or, laftly, if it
was the Word of God, and not the Son, who
came down from Heaven to be incarnate; if
fo fignal a tranfition, from being the Word
to being the Son of God, had taken place
during the interval of his defcenfion and af-
cenfion, how could St. Paul affert *, " He
" that defcended is the fame alfo that af-
" cended ?" But enough on the proof from
St. John.

Another reafon which induces Mr. Hawtrey to think that the Filiation then took
place, when the λόγος σὰρξ ἐγένετο, is derived
from the language of the angel to the Virgin
Mary *. Now till it is proved that no Hebrew

" John c. xiv. v. 11. x. 30, 38. xvii. 21.
* John c. v. ver. 26.   ʸ Ephef. c. iv. v. 10.
ᶻ Luke i. 25.
" Therefore, then, it may be concluded, the title, *Son of*
" God, would be when this event fhould have taken place, and,
" of

idioms have crept into St. Luke's ftyle, it will not neceffarily follow that any idea of *title* is implied in κληθήσεται. This however, though it may make a change in the form of the fyllogifm neceffary, will not materially affect the proof, nor render it inconclufive, if it was not fo before. But as the Catholic Church holds that it was the Son of God that was made flefh, and that *after* his myfterious union with human nature he was ftill the Son of God, it is evident that the words of the Angel are as applicable to our creed as to Mr. Hawtrey's. And this for the prefent may fuffice; as we fhall have occafion again to notice this verfe, when we produce the teftimony of Novatian.

The remaining fcriptural proof, or to fpeak more accurately, the remaining * text for confideration is that, for the interpretation of which Mr. Hawtrey's digreffion on the Filiation feems to have been introduced. His expofition of this text feems, if I do not mifapprehend it, to lead to confequences which could not efcape his obfervation; and yet the force of which, if they were obferved,

---

" of courfe, that in the birth of the λόγος in union with the σάρξ " ἀνθρωπίνη, confifted the Filiation, and, confequently, that there " was no Filiation prior to that event." Θεάνθρωπος, p. 40.

* 1 Cor. xv. 28.

could not but be fenfibly felt. On this account, I confefs, I feel more apprehenfion that I may have confidered it in a miftaken point of view, than conviction that I am right. " Then," fays he [b], (in his paraphrafe on the Apoftle's words, " then fhall the Son " himfelf be fubject unto him that put all " things under him") " fhall the difpenfation " of Θεάνθρωπος be terminated, and the union " of the λόγος with man's nature ceafe." If now, according to Mr. Hawtrey's hypothefis, the Son is a compound of the λόγος and man's nature; and if, according to Mr. Hawtrey's paraphrafe, the union of the λόγος with man's nature is to ceafe, it appears an obvious inference that the Son is to ceafe alfo. Strange! that the beloved Son of God, over whom, we are told, death hath no more dominion, fhould ceafe to exift, at a time when the graves have given up their dead; and that he himfelf fhould be doomed to annihilation, at the very moment, when thofe whom he has ranfomed, are bid to enter into the joy of their Lord! The Sibylline oracle fpeaks a language more confiftent with our firft notions of the Son of God, and more truly defcriptive of the vital effence of a divine Being.

[b] Θεάνθρωπος, p. 38.

E:

Εἰ δὲ γὲ γεννῶσιν, καὶ Ἀθάνατοί γε μίνετι [e].

This difficulty, arifing from the ceffation of the Son, might in fome degree be removed, if we were to confider him as an adopted Son : but this again is repugnant to other parts of Mr. Hawtrey's fcheme ; and is indeed a herefy, which we are fure he never would countenance, as the cloyftered fcholars, even in the dark period of the Heptarchy, had theology enough to confute it [d]. Nor is this the only difficulty with which this hypothefis is encumbered; for it inclines, I think, to favour the doctrine of a phyfical generation. He, who afferts that the λόγος became υἱὸς in confequence of the Incarnation, feems to imply that that Relationfhip originated, not altogether indeed in the fame mode, becaufe a fupernatural Interpofition is ftill admitted, but yet in fome fort of refemblance to that Nativity, which gives rife to the fame Relationfhip as it fubfifts amongft Men. A doctrine, which tends thus to degrade the Son of God to a level with the reft of the creation, was combated, as we have feen, with peculiar ability, by the ancient Commentators on St. John. In fhort, this hypothefis, which was intended as far as

[e] Apud Theoph. Antioch. p. 49.
[d] Hume's Hift. of England, p. 35. Ed. 4to.

D

the

the nature of the fubject would admit, to fimplify a myftery, feems only to entangle it in greater perplexities.

Before we clofe our fcriptural review of the Doctrine, the Silence of the other Evangelifts on this fingular diftinction of characters ought to be noticed. For if St. Matthew had underftood that Chrift's Filiation commenced only at his Nativity on earth, would he not, whilft unfolding his genealogy, and afferting the operation of the Holy Spirit, would he not have embraced the opportunity, fo peculiarly adapted to the purpofe, of informing us that he then *firft* began to exift in the relative capacity of the Son of God ? If that had really been the era of a *new* relation which Chrift was to bear to God, is it probable that he would have omitted fo interefting a point of information ? And does not on the contrary the direct and abrupt manner in which St. Mark introduces " the " Gofpel of Jefus Chrift," whom, without any reference to his lineage or any allufion to his Incarnation, he ftyles fimply and abftractedly the Son of God, feem to indicate that his Filiation was coeval with his eternal exiftence ? This at leaft feems probable, that if his Incarnation had been the *original caufe* of his Sonfhip, neither would St. Matthew, when

when relating the one, have omitted the other : nor would St. Mark, without noticing his birth, the fufpected origin of fo extraordinary a connexion, have called him the Son of God, unlefs that Sonfhip had exifted antecedently to that birth. This, however, is but conjectural reafoning, though highly probable I think ; but as we have much more fubftantial ground to reft upon, I do not infift upon it—valeat, quantum valore poteft.

After having endeavoured thus to afcertain the information which Revelation gives us on the fubject, it will be neither an uninterefting nor an unprofitable fpeculation to extend our inquiry to the writings of the Fathers.

The importance of the argument, derived from the fentiments of the primitive Chriftians, is fufficiently proved from the eagernefs, with which controverfialifts of every fect refort to them ; and if any thing further were wanting to vindicate their value, we fhould find it amply fupplied in the learned labours of Dodwell, Grabe, and Bull. To the affiftance, however, of the early Apologifts of Chriftianity, Mr. Hawtrey has not directly had recourfe ; though by introducing the negative teftimony of the Nicene Creed corrected, or rather by expunging its pofitive evidence, in what he deems its interpolated

ftate,

ftate, he has acknowledged and reafoned upon the fame principle on which an appeal to the Fathers is founded. For he would not, I conceive, have adverted at all to a Council holden in the three hundred and twenty fifth year of the Chriftian era, unlefs he had confidered the refult of the pious deliberations of that Council as an epitome of the prevailing fentiments of the three firft centuries. Had not the doctrine of the Council of Nice been in unifon with the doctrine of the preceding ages, Mr. Hawtrey would naturally have paid little regard to it's authority : fo that the force of the argument, whatever it be, deducible from the Nicene Creed, is dependant upon, and ultimately refolvable into, its coincidence with the doctrine maintained by the fucceffors of the Apoftles down to the time of Conftantine. To them therefore our attention is of courfe directed ; and after having adduced their fentiments on the fubject of our inquiry, we will refume our comment on the Nicene Creed ; and fhall be able, I think, to fhew, that whether the fufpected claufe had or had not the fanction of the Council is not very material ; not only becaufe the unvarying uniformity of opinion, which pervades the works of the Fathers of the three firft centuries, in a great

meafure

measure superfedes the want of that evidence which the authority of a General Council would supply ; but becaufe there are other parts in the Creed unqueftionably genuine, which imply, if they do not exprefs, the doctrine of the Eternal Filiation.

Beginning with the Fathers of the Apof-tolical age, we will introduce the reft in the order in which they are ufually fuppofed to have flourifhed ; thus fhewing how the evidence of antiquity flows in an uninterrupted ftream from the days of Barnabas down to the fourth century.

I would, however, firft premife, that no advantage will, or indeed can, be taken of any paffages, in which the eternity of the λόγος is afferted, be it in terms of perfonification ever fo ftrong and peremptory. For *before* the Identity of the Word and the Son is demonftrated to have been maintained by them from a comprehenfive view of their fentiments, fuch proofs, in order to be pertinent and conclufive, would involve an af-fumption of a doubtful point ; and *after* it is demonftrated, they would be fuperfluous.

St. Barnabas, in the firft Greek chapter that is preferved to us of his Epiftle (the fifth including thofe that are loft) is enume-rating fome of the caufes of our Saviour's

D 3

Advent,

Advent, and says, ἥκων ὁ υἱὸς τῦ Θεῦ ἐς τοῦτο ἦλθεν ἐν σαρκί. Now upon every principle of fair interpretation, these words certainly imply, that our Saviour was the *Son* of God, *before* he came in the flesh. The holy Father would not have been justified in so far anticipating the relation which Christ was to bear to God in consequence of his Incarnation, as to say the *Son* of God came in the flesh, if that coming in the flesh was the *cause* of his becoming the *Son*. For, if that had been the case, it would not have been the *Son* that came in the flesh, but somebody else ; ὁ λόγος or τὶ πνεῦμα : so that these words taken in their plain and obvious sense assert the doctrine of a Filiation prior to the Incarnation. And nearly parallel with this passage is another, which will illustrate and confirm our interpretation of this : ἐχ' ὁ υἱὸς ἀνθρώπω, ἀλλ' ὁ υἱὸς τῦ Θεῦ τυπῷ καὶ ἐν σαρκὶ φανερωθείς[e]. There is still one other passage to be quoted from this celebrated Epistle, which shews that the Author of it believed the Filiation to be at least antecedent to the creation of Man. It is in the sixth chapter, where, before he cites those words of the Almighty, "·Let " us make man[f]," he says, ὡς λέγει τῷ υἱῷ ;

---

[e] Barnab. Epist. c. xii.   [f] Gen. i. 26.

and

after having cited them, he adds, ταῦτα πρὸς τὸν υἱόν.

We muſt not be ſurpriſed if we find in Hermas little that bears upon our Queſtion. Often obſcure and myſtical, and intent rather upon inculcating moral and religious precepts to regulate the practice than doctrines to exerciſe the faith, there are few points of controverſial Divinity that can derive confirmation from him. There is, however, one paſſage which directly applies to the article in diſpute. " Filius quidem Dei omni creaturâ " antiquior eſt, ita ut in conſilio Patri ſuo " adfuerit, ad condendam creaturam [e]."

In Ignatius' Epiſtle to the Magneſians we have a paſſage ſomething ſimilar to this of Hermas. Ὅς (ſcil. Χριςὸς) πρὸ αἰώνων παρὰ ΠΑΤΡΙ ἦν [h]. If Ignatius had meant that this eternal exiſtence was in the character of λόγος and not υἱὸς, he would probably have uſed the word Θεῷ and not Πατρὶ, which, as a relative term, ſo naturally ſuggeſts the correſponding idea of Son. That one of his Commentators underſtood him to mean this, is clear from his annotation on the paſſage ; " utpote æterni Patris æternus Filius [i]." And with this agrees the Commentary of the ve-

e Hermæ Paſtor, 1. iii. c. 12.   h c. 6.
i In Ignat. Epiſt. gen. Schol. p. 78. edit. a T. Smith.

tus Theologus, on the 19th chapter of Ignatius' Epiftle to the Ephefians, as quoted by Voffius, and who, he feems to think, was Jerome or Ambrofe. " Dei *Filius* in utero " Virginis *incarnari* voluit [k]."

To overlook the proofs contained in the interpolated epiftles of Ignatius, as we fhould not want a precedent for quoting them in great and learned men, may be thought an important omiffion. To the force of ὃς πρὸ αἰῶνος παρὰ τῷ Πατρὶ γεννηθεὶς in his Epiftle to the Magnefians ; and of τὸν πρὸ αἰώνων υἱὸν μονογενῆ καὶ λόγον in that to the Ephefians, to the force of thefe expreffions it were impoffible to be infenfible. But as we have already, I think, fhewn Ignatius' fentiments from a text undoubtedly genuine, it feemed not neceffary to be tenacious of paffages, the authenticity of which was fufpected, and that fufpicion too avowed by fuch a hoft of Critics.

What weight the Conftitutiones Apoftolicæ ought to have in regulating our decifion, I leave to others to determine ; but muft remark that Bifhop Bull quotes [1] Cardinal Bo-

[k] Patres Apoftol. tom. ii. p. 16. Ed. Cotel.
[1] " Quicquid fit de Auctore harum Conftitutionum, certum " tamen apud omnes atque exploratum nunc eft, quòd Confilio " Nicæno antiquiores fint." Judic. Ecclef. Cath. de neceff. &c. p. 50. Ed. Grabe.

na's

na's opinion, and fays other very learned
men agreed with him, that they were older
than the Council of Nice. As there are in
them feveral paffages which indirectly affert
the Eternal Generation, fo there is one which
avows it in plain and explicit terms. The
Jews are accufed of blindnefs for not believing Chrift to be the only begotten Son of
God, begotten before all ages [m].

Again; fubmitting it to others to appre-
ciate the credit of the Recognitiones Cle-
mentis, I would obferve that it is there faid,
He who was *already* the Son of God, and the
beginning of all things, was made Man [n].

If the References we have made to the
Apoftolical Fathers be thought few, they
muft at leaft be allowed to be unequivocal;
and if to us, who affert the Eternal Filiation,
be objected the poverty of the fupport to be
derived from their writings; to thofe who
deny it may more fairly be imputed the total
abfence of primitive Authority. As often as
any expreffion occurs that at all affects our
Inquiry, it is decifive in our favour; and that

---

[m] Ἀδλειψία γὰρ αὐτοῖς κατεχύθη διὰ τὴν κακόνοιαν αὐτῶν, ὅτι βλέποντες τὸν Ἰησοῦν ἐκ ἐπίςευον αὐτὸν εἶναι τὸν Χριςὸν τῦ Θεῦ, τὸν ΠΡΟ
ΠΑΝΤΩΝ ΑΙΩΝΩΝ ΕΞ ΑΥΤΟΥ ΓΕΝΝΗΘΕΝΤΑ, υἱὸν μονογενῆ,
λόγον Θεὸν, κ. τ. λ. Conftit. Apol. l. v. c. 16. p. 314. tom. i.
Ed. Cotel.

[n] *Cum effet Filius* Dei, et initium omnium, homo factus effet. Recog. S. Clem. l. i. p. 503. tom. i. Ed. Cotel.

fuch

fuch expreffions are not more frequent and more explicit is owing probably to caufes, which their own writings themfelves enable us to affign. For in them we find they had many and complicated fubjects of vaft importance at once preffing on their minds. They had to convince the Judaizing Chriftians of the abrogation of the ceremonial Law, and yet to caution them from running into the oppofite extreme of a merely fpeculative and barren Faith. They had to animate their new converts amidft the rage of Perfecution, by placing before them the unfhaken conftancy of fuffering Patriarchs, and the ftill brighter example of a fuffering Saviour. They had to recommend a fyftem of Ecclefiaftical Government, formed on the outline of their bleffed Mafter's inftructions, and fo modelled as to command reverence, and enfure tranquillity to the Church. Thus their primary object clearly was to eradicate inveterate prejudices, to fettle the fundamental principles of Chriftianity, and to provide for the dignified order of the Church : and if it was a fecondary object with them to combat Herefies, we may fay, without excluding proleptic refutations of future Herefies, that they would be principally fuch as then exifted. Of thofe points therefore on which

which no difference in their days or their diſtrict prevailed, we muſt not expect to find any laboured defence, but at the moſt only incidental proofs : and ſuch, we conceive, are the Quotations we have made from Barnabas, Hermas and Ignatius.

But when, in progreſs of time, thoſe ſame points became the topics of controverſy and the cauſes of ſchiſm, we may then reaſonably expect a more ample detail of argument. Nor will our expectation be diſappointed ; for in the Fathers of the ſecond and third Century we find abundant materials to prove, that they believed the Eternal Exiſtence of the *Son* to be the Doctrine of the Scriptures.

In the two Apologies of Juſtin Martyr, written, as they were, with a view to vindicate the profeſſors of the Chriſtian Faith, there muſt almoſt of neceſſity be contained an explanation of what that Faith was. Independently of the profeſſed object of theſe two Apologies, as he was addreſſing perſons unacquainted with the very elements of Chriſtianity, a Heathen Emperor and the unconverted Senate of Rome ; in theſe I ſay, as well as in his Dialogue with the unbelieving Jew ; as they were addreſſed to thoſe whom he would of courſe feel anxious to inſtruct in the genuine doctrines of the Goſpel, we may hope

hope to find the real tenets of uncorrupted Chriſtianity. When therefore ſuch expreſſions as theſe, "that it was the *Son* who "ſpoke to Moſes [o];" that "the *Son* of God, "he who is alone properly called Son, the "Word exiſted together with God, and was "*begotten* before all created things [p];" and again, "aſſerting him to be the Son, we un"derſtand him to have come forth from the "Father before all things that are made [q];" — when theſe expreſſions are deliberately weighed, expreſſions not caſually dropt, but introduced again and again, and accompanied with long and laboured explanations, the unprejudiced Inquirer will be fully ſatisfied that Juſtin maintained the Eternal Filiation; and may poſſibly be diſpoſed to think that he maintained it, becauſe he had received it from higher and more unerring authority.

That the teſtimony of Irenæus, the ſcholar of Polycarp, is equally ſtrong will appear from the conſideration of the following paſſages. "This Father," ſays he, "of our

[o] Τῦ λαλήσαντος αὐτῷ ὄντος ΥΙΟΥ τῦ Θεῦ. Apol. prim. p. 94. Ed. Thirlby.

[p] Ὁ δὲ υἱὸς ἐκείνυ, ὁ μόνος λεγόμενος κυρίως υἱὸς, ὁ λόγος πρὸ τῶν ποιημάτων καὶ συνὼν καὶ γεννώμενος. Apol. ſecund. p. 115.

[q] Υἱὸν αὐτὸν λέγοντες, νενοήκαμεν ὄντα καὶ πρὸ πάντων ποιημάτων ἀπὸ τῦ Πατρὸς δυνάμει καὶ βυλῇ προελθόντα. Dialog. p. 353.

Τῦτο τὸ τῷ ὄντι ἀπὸ τῦ Πατρὸς προβληθὲν γέννημα πρὸ πάντων τῶν ποιημάτων συνῆν τῷ Πατρὶ, κ. τ. λ. Dial. p. 270.

"Lord

" Lord Jefus Chrift is revealed——by his
" Word, who is his *Son*. Now the Son, al-
" *ways co*-exifting with the Father, long fince
" and from the beginning reveals the Father,
" &c. '" " He is the only-begotten of the
" Father, the Word of God, *incarnate*, when
" the fulnefs of time was come, in which
" the *Son of God* was to become the Son of
" Man '." The 20th and 21ft Chapters of
the 3d Book abound with proofs of the Son's
Eternity ; in the former of which he replies
to the cavil, fi natus eft, non erat ante Chrif-
tus, " oftendimus non *tunc* coepit Filius Dei
" exiftens *femper* apud Patrem ;" and a little
while after he afferts, that " the *Son*, the
" Word of God, defcended from his Father,
" and was made *incarnate* '." But it is unneceffary to accumulate proofs from tho
fame Author ; and we fhall better demon-
ftrate the univerfal prevalence of the Doctrine

' Hic Pater Domini noftri Jefu Chrifti, per verbum fuum,
qui eft Filius ejus, per eum revelatur et manifeftatur omnibus,
quibus revelatur.—Semper autem co-exiftens Filius Patri, olim
et ab-initio femper revelat Patrem, &c. Irenæ. adverfus Hæ-
ref. l. ii. c. 55. p. 185. Ed. Grabe.
    Again p. 333. Enarrat ergo *ab initio* Filius Patris quippe
qui ab initio eft cum Patre, &c.
    ' Unigenitus Patris,—et verbum Dei, incarnatus, cum ad-
veniffet plenitudo temporis, in quo Filium hominis fieri opor-
tebat Filium Dei. l. iii. c. 18. p. 242.
    ' *Filius*, Verbum Dei exiftens, a Patre defcendens et incarna-
tus. p. 245.

we are contending for by introducing feveral witneffes than by extending the teftimony of one. We muft not however take leave of Irenæus without obferving on the title of his work,——adverfus Hærefes. For the natural inference is that he was fully perfuaded the doctrine of the Eternal Filiation was founded in Scripture; as into a work, in which he was labouring to eradicate the inveterate errors of Valentinus and the Gnoftics, he would be particularly cautious that no new one fhould gain admiffion.

A well known paffage in Theophilus ᵉ, though it is couched in terms more congenial with the creed of Plato than the language of Revelation, yet contains fome affertions not irrelevant to our point. For if the author does not infift on the Eternal Generation, he does however on one prior to the Creation ; and that Generation too is predicated both of υἱὸς and λόγος. If he does not exactly fay the Filiation of the Son of God was ab

---

ᵉ Ὁ λόγος ὁ τῦ Θεῦ, ὅς ἐςι ἡ ΥΙΟΣ αὐτῦ· ὐχ ὡς οἱ ποιηταὶ καὶ μυθογράφοι λέγεσι υἱὲς θεῶν ἐκ συνεσίας γιννωμένες, ἀλλὰ ὡς ἀλήθεια διηγεῖται τὸν λόγον, τὸν ὄντα διαπαντὸς ἐνδιάθετον ἐν καρδίᾳ Θεῦ. πρὸ γάρ τι γίνεσθαι τῦτον εἶχε σύμβελον ἑαυτῦ τῦν, καὶ φρόνησιν ὄντα· ὁπότε δὲ ἠθέλησεν ὁ Θεὸς ποιῆσαι ὅσα ἐβελεύσαλο, τῦτον τὸν λόγον ΕΓΕΝΝΗΣΕ προφορικὸν, πρωτότοκον πάσης κτίσεως, ἰ κενωθεὶς αὐτὸς τῦ λόγυ, ἀλλὰ λόγον ΓΕΝΝΗΣΑΣ, κỳ τῷ λόγῳ αὐτῦ διαπαιδὸς ὁμιλῶν. Theoph. l. ii. p. 129. Ed. Ox. and again p. 130. Θεὸς ἂν ὢν ὁ λόγος, καὶ ἐκ Θεῦ πεφυκὼς, κ. τ. λ.

æterno,

æterno, he yet inculcates the *identity* of υἱὸς and λόγος, whom he affirms to have been eternal, and, by afferting a *Generation* before the Almighty created the world, afferts, by implication at leaft, the previous exiftence of the *Son*. Not Theophilus only, but many of the Fathers fpeak of the Son's going forth to create the world, as of a Generation. In fact, as has been often fhewn, they apply the general term of Generation to his Eternal Emanation from the Father, to his agency in the creation of the world, and to his Nativity. But it muft be allowed of them all, that, as they affert, that he was eternally begotten by the Father, the word Generation could only be applied by them to the two laft Events in a qualified and fubordinate fenfe [x]. And with regard to Theophilus in particular, as he here declares that the λόγος always was with God, and that that *fame* λόγος was the Son, not λόγος σαρκωθεὶς or λόγος ἐνανθρωπήσας, but λόγος in its primitive and abfolute meaning, independently of any fuperinduced nature; we certainly have his authority for infifting on the Eternal Generation, or what amounts to the fame thing, the eternal exiftence of the *Son*.

[x] Vera et propria Filii generatio ea fola eft, quæ ex Deo Patre, ut mentis ipfius æternæ productio, ex æterno extitit. Bullii Defenf. Fid. Nic. p. 208.

Athena-

Athenagoras, after having explained to the Emperors Marcus Aurelius Antoninus and Lucius Aurelius Commodus, the Chriſtian's notion of God, tells them that belief in the *Son* of God alſo makes part of a Chriſtian's creed; and proceeds to inform them what he underſtood by Son. "The Son," ſays he, "is the Word of God in idea and energy; "for by *him* and through *him* were all things "made, the Father and the Son being one[y]." Again he calls him "the *firſt offspring* of the "Father, not as having been made;" and goes on to elucidate his meaning by language borrowed from the Platonic Philoſophy. Here then, whatever obſcurity may have ariſen from a mixture of philoſophical and evangelical language, here I ſay, as alſo in other parts of his Defence[z], we find aſſerted the eternal ex-

[y] Νοοῦμεν γὰρ καὶ υἱὸν τοῦ Θεοῦ.—ἔστιν ὁ υἱὸς τοῦ Θεοῦ λόγος τοῦ Πατρὸς, ἐν ἰδέᾳ καὶ ἐνεργείᾳ. On theſe laſt words, when they occur ſoon after in the Apology, Biſhop Horſley remarks, "Here indeed "the Son of God is called an idea and an energy. But it is "not to be underſtood that he is an unſubſtantial idea, or ener-"gy, of the paternal mind; but a living idea energizing on "the matter of the univerſe to ſtamp it with the forms of "things." Controverſial Tracts, p. 57. But Athenagoras proceeds, πρὸς αὐτοῦ γὰρ καὶ δι' αὐτοῦ πάντα ἐγένετο, ἑνὸς ὄντος τοῦ Πατρὸς καὶ τοῦ υἱοῦ· ὄντος δὲ τοῦ υἱοῦ ἐν Πατρὶ, καὶ Πατρὸς ἐν υἱῷ, ἑνότητι καὶ δυνάμει πνεύματος, νοῦς καὶ λόγος τοῦ Πατρὸς, ὁ υἱὸς τοῦ Θεοῦ. Εἰ δὲ δι' ὑπερβολὴν συνέσεως σκοπεῖν ὑμῖν ἔπεισιν, ὁ παῖς τί βούλεται, ἐρῶ διὰ βραχέων· πρῶτον γέννημα εἶναι τῷ Πατρὶ, οὐχ ὡς γενόμενον· κ. τ. λ. Athenag. Leg. p. 38. Ed. Ox. 1682.

[z] Ἑνὶ τῷ Θεῷ καὶ τῷ παρ' αὐτοῦ λόγῳ υἱῷ νοουμένῳ ἀμερίστῳ πάντα ὑποτέτακται. p. 70.

iſtence

iftence of the Son, and his original Identity
with the λόγος, by one who was of the
number of thofe, ὑπὲρ ΑΛΗΘΕΙΑΣ ἀόκνως καὶ
τὰς ψυχὰς ἐπιδιδόντες [*]. It may too be worth
remarking that Athenagoras enumerates the
Perfons in the bleffed Trinity by the names
of Father, Son, and Spirit [*]. Now if he had
thought the *Son* was a title expreffive of only
a temporary relation, which commenced at the
Incarnation, and was to terminate at the final
confummation of all things, it is not at all
probable that he would under a name expreffive of fuch a tranfitory character have
defcribed him as co-exifting with the Father,
and the Spirit, who never had a beginning,
and can never have an end.

It is of no confequence that we do not
find the precife phrafes Eternal Filiation or
Eternal Generation in the Ante-Nicene Fathers, as long as we find in them expreffions
tantamount to thefe words. Nor is the
adoption of that phrafeology by the Poft-Ni-

---

[*] p. 17.
[*] Τίς ἡ ϖ παιδὸς ϖρὸς τὸν Πατέρα ἑνότης, τίς ἡ ϖ Πατρὸς ϖρὸς τὸν
υἱὸν κοινωνία, τὶ τὸ πνεῦμα, τίς ἡ ϖ τοσούτων ἕνωσις, καὶ διαίρεσις ἑνω-
μένων, ϖ Πνεύματος, ϖ Παιδὸς, ϖ Πατρός. p. 49.
Ὡς γὰρ Θεὸν φαμεν, καὶ υἱὸν τὸν λόγον αὐτῶ, κỳ Πνεῦμα ἅγιον, ἑνώ-
μενα μ᾽ κατὰ δύναμιν, τὸν Πατέρα, τὸν Υἱὸν, τὸ Πνεῦμα. κ. τ. λ. p.
110. So too Tertullian ; " unus Deus, ex quo et gradus ifti
" et formæ et fpecies in nomine Patris, et Filii, et Spiritus
" fancti." Adverf. Prax. p. 501. Ed. Par.

E   ceno

cene Fathers any more convincing proof that they believed in the doctrine, than what we have of their predeceffors having done the fame. The truth is that till a queftion affumes the ferious afpect of controverfy, a writer does not think of clothing his ideas in the technical language of controverfial precifion. Thus when Clemens Alexandrinus fays that the Son is eternal and without a beginning[c], he muft be underftood to fpeak of his Generation: for in another place he declares him to be God, in confequence of his being *Son*[d]. Now as the Godhead afcribed to him cannot but be allowed to be *eternal*; fo it muft too, I think, be allowed, that Clemens would never have affigned his Filiation as the *caufe* of that Godhead, unlefs he had believed it to be *eternal* too.

It is unneceffary to refer to the occafional proofs which are interfperfed in Novatian's treatife " de Regula Fidei;" as there is one whole Chapter, in which, whilft he is refuting a herefy founded, as he fufpects, on a mifconception of that very verfe in St. Luke[e]

---

[c] Ἐν δὲ τοῖς νοητοῖς, τὸ πρισβύτερον ἐν γενέσει, τὴν ἄχρονον ἀναρχον ἀρχήν τε καὶ ἀπαρχὴν τῶν ὄντων, τὸν υἱόν. Clem. Alex. Strom. l. vii. p. 829. Ed. Potter.

[d] Ὁ φανερώτατος ὄντως Θεὸς, ὁ τῷ Δεσπότη τῶν ὅλων ἐξισωθεὶς,— ΟΤΙ ἦν υἱὸς αὐτῷ, κ. τ. λ. Clem. Alex. Cohort. ad Gent. p. 86.

[e] i. 35.

which

which is preſſed into the ſupport of Mr.
Hawtrey's Hypotheſis, he maintains the prior
exiſtence of the incarnate Word, in the capacity of the *Son* of God. They, we find,
who denied any diſtinction between the Son
of Man and the Son of God, uſed to allege,
in confirmation of their doctrine, the words
of the Angel to the Virgin Mary. " The
" Holy Ghoſt ſhall come upon thee, and the
" power of the Higheſt ſhall overſhadow
" thee: therefore alſo that Holy thing which
" ſhall be born of thee ſhall be called the
" Son of God." Their Commentary upon
the text, and their inference run thus. Since,
ſay they, that Holy thing which the Angel
tells Mary ſhall be called the Son of God,
is the ſubſtance of fleſh and blood, brought
forth by Mary; and ſince the Angel declared
that that which was born of her ſhould be
the Son of God, it follows that a very Man
is the Son of God [f]. Novatian in reply ob-
ſerves, that the Scriptures ſay that Holy
thing ALSO, intending by the conjunction *et*
to ſhew that ſomething elſe too was the Son

---

[f] Si ergo, inquiunt, Angelus Dei dicit ad Mariam, " quod
" ex te naſcetur ſanctum," ex Maria eſt ſubſtantia carnis et
corporis ; hanc autem ſubſtantiam, i. e. ſanctum hoc, quod ex
illa genitum eſt, *Filium* Dei eſſe propoſuit : Homo, inquiunt,
ipſe et illa caro corporis, illud quod ſanctum eſt dictum, ipſum
eſt *Filius* Dei. Novat. Lib. de Reg. Fid. c. 24.

of

of God; that the offspring of Mary was fo
in a derived and fecondary fenfe; but that
the *Word* of God was fo in a primary and
higher fenfe [s]. Mr. Hawtrey's opinion, I am
aware, differs materially from the heretical
one here combated: but as he fuppofes the
Filiation to have confifted only in the Incarnation, this Chapter, which teaches that the
Word of God exifted as *Son*, before his af-
fumption of human Nature, is equally fub-
verfive of both. There are, it may perhaps
be faid, fome paffages in Novatian for which
he may be taxed with believing in the exiftence of the Word prior to that of the
Son; and his language in the 31ft chapter
in particular may be urged as juftifying the
imputation. Under certain reftrictions we
allow it; but muft deny that he there at all
favours the fuppofition of the Filiation being coeval only with the Incarnation. After
having declared the Being of one God, his
words are; " ex quo (fcil. Deo) quando ipfe
" voluit, Sermo Filius natus eft." But if we
confider Filius as put in appofition with Ser-

---

[s] Ait enim (fcil. Scriptura) propterea. ET *quod ex te nafcetur
fanctum*, ut illud oftenderet, non principaliter hoc fanctum,
quod ex illa nafcitur,——Filium Dei effe, fed confequenter et in
fecundo loco: principaliter autem *Filium* Dei effe *Verbum* Dei,
incarnatum per illum fpiritum——Hic eft enim legitimus Dei
Filius qui ex *ipfo* Deo eft.

mo,

mo, the feeming inconfiftency of this with other paffages is removed; and perhaps the words which follow, " hic ergo, cum fit geni- " tus a Patre, femper eft in Patre," may be thought to countenance this conftruction. But be this as it may; if it fhall be thought that Novatian, with many of the Platonic fchool, taught that a Filiation took place, when the eternal Word was produced or ge- nerated by the paternal will for the great work of creation, it muft ftill be granted that he believed fuch Filiation to have pre- ceded the Incarnation; and muft be under- ftood in the fame limited fenfe as the paf- fage noticed in Theophilus.

Tertullian, in his Apology adverfus Gentes, fhews us that he thought the Word and the Son the fame; and whilft he afferts the Eter- nal Generation, he adds, naturally enough, that it was the reafon why he was called *Son.* " Hunc (fcil. Sermonem) ex *Deo* pro- " latum didicimus, et prolatione *generatum,* " et idcirco Filium Dei, et Deum dictum ex " unitate fubftantiæ [b]. Again; in his trea- tife De carne Chrifti, he fpeaks of him, who being *already* the *Son* of God, affumed hu- man Nature in order to become the Son of

[b] P. 19. Ed. Par. 1675.

E 3

Man.

Man [i]. But, leaving thefe detached paffages, let us advert to his comprehenfive Refutation of the herefy of Praxeas. It cannot be diffembled that here too there are parts, which favour the idea of a Generation, immediately preceding the Creation. But then again, independently of the paffages juft quoted, as he believed in the eternity of the Holy Spirit, and taught that he proceeded from the Father and the Son, he muft a fortiori have believed, that the Son was eternal; and this term Generation could only have been ufed by him as expreffive of a tranfition from a ftate of comparative quiefcence to one of exertion and activity. If the [k] paffage in his book contra Hermogenem be adduced to prove that he believed the Filiation to be only temporal, we reply with [l] Bifhop Bull, that if he really taught this, he was a Heretic. Tertullian, it is well known, did fometimes play the Heretic; but in this cafe, I fhould rather think he meant Son in his *hu-*

---

[i] Ergo, *jam* Dei *Filius* ex Patris Dei femine, i. e. fpiritu, ut effet *et* hominis *Filius,* caro ei fola erat ex hominis carne fumenda. p. 321.

[k] Quia et Pater Deus eft, et judex Deus eft, non tamen ideo Pater et judex femper, quia Deus femper. Nam nec Pater potuit effe ante Filium, nec judex ante delictum. Fuit autem tempus, cum et delictum et Filius non fuit, quod Judicem, et qui Patrem Dominum faceret. cap. iii.

[l] Defenf. Fid. Nic. p. 235.

man capacity. Bifhop Bull, I am aware, re-
probates the conjecture of Bellarmin (who
thought Filius was to be underftood of any
holy man, who was the child of God by
adoption), and feems inclined to attribute it
to downright heterodoxy. Bold muft he
be, who can differ from Bifhop Bull without feeling that his heart mifgives him.
But yet as Delictum is here coupled with
Filius, and as it was for the purpofe of
wafhing away that Delictum by his own
blood that he became Filius in his human
capacity, I think it not impoffible that Tertullian meant what I have ventured to fuppofe. At all events, it is not to be reconciled
with his affertions elfewhere, to fuppofe that
he ever dreamt of the Word being the Son
of God *only* in confequence of his affumption
of human Nature. For, when he was grap-
pling with the herefy of Praxeas, which confifted in the affirmation of fo ftrict an Unity
of Father and Son, as to involve the cruci-
fixion of the Father as a neceffary confequence of the Son's ; would he not, had he
thought the pofition tenable, have at once
demolifhed this herefy by declaring the phyfical Impoffibility of fuch an Unity between
a Father who exifted from all eternity, and

E 4

a Son

a Son who, as such, only existed from his
Incarnation ? I may further ask, is it not
more than probable, that Praxeas' heresy
arose from a confusion of ideas which crowd-
ed on his mind, whilst reflecting on the co-
eternity of the Father and the Son ? This argument indeed, founded on the reply which
Tertullian does not make, as it is only a negative one ; and this conjecture of the probable
source of Praxeas' heresy, may, after the introduction of direct and positive evidence, be
thought superfluous. But the fact, I think, of
Tertullian's silence strongly marks both his
own sentiments, and the current doctrine of
the Age.

Though the evidence already brought for-
wards may be thought sufficient to demon-
strate what the Faith of the Ante-Nicene Fathers was ; yet there are some other names,
which it may be as well briefly to enumerate,
in order to shew the unbroken series of our
authorities.

Methodius, it will be allowed, could not
have ascribed to the *Son* any share in the
creation of the world, if he had not believed
in his pre-existence in that capacity ; and
that he does ascribe to him such cooperation
is evident. Ἐϛι δὲ ὁ υἱὸς, ἡ παντοδύναμος καὶ
κραταιὰ

κρατικωτάτη χεὶρ τοῦ Πατρὸς, ἐν ᾗ μετὰ τὸ ποιῆσαι τὴν ὕλην ἐξ οὐκ ὄντων κατακοσμεῖ [m]. Again; he defcribes the Son as himfelf communicating to the Prophets his future advent in the flefh [n]. And laftly, he fays, the Almighty faid to him, Thou art my Son, ἐμφαίνων μήτε ΠΡΟΣΦΑΤΟΝ αὐτὸν τετυχηκέναι τῆς υἱοθεσίας, μήτε αὖ ΠΡΟϋπάρξοντα τέλος ἐσχηκέναι· ἀλλὰ εἶναι ἀεὶ τὸν αὐτόν [o].

Hippolytus efteems it one of the free gifts of God, to believe that he, who *before the worlds* was the *only-begotten*, was afterwards born of a Virgin [p].

Gregory of Neocæfarea, in his Expofitio Fidei, calls him an eternal Son of an eternal Father; and fays that the Father was never without the Son, nor the Son without the Spirit [q].

Theodotus defcribes πρωτότοκος as γεννηθεὶς ἀπαθῶς, κτίστης καὶ γενεσιάρχης τῆς ὅλης ἐγένετο κτίσεώς τε καὶ οὐσίας [r].

I cannot quit the Fathers without again adverting to the triple Filiation which fome

[m] Photii Biblioth. p. 937. Ed. Schott.

[n] Ibid. p. 957. [o] Ibid. p. 960.

[p] Ὅτι εὐδοκίᾳ Θεοῦ, ὁ πρὸ αἰώνων μονογενὴς ἐν ὑστέρῳ καιρῷ ἐκ παρθένου γεγένηται, κ. τ. λ. De charifm. trad. Apoft. p. 246. Ed. Fabric.

[q] Ἀΐδιος ἀϊδίου—Οὔτε ἂν ἐνέλειπέ ποτε υἱὸς Πατρὶ, οὔτε υἱῷ πνεῦμα, κ. τ. λ. Fabric. Bib. Græc. p. 250. tom. 5.

[r] Ibid. p. 146. tom. 5.

of

of them taught; as it will give me an opportunity of introducing Dr. Waterland's fentiments on the fubject, and of drawing the
line of demarkation between Mr. Hawtrey
and thofe of them who approached neareft
to his fyftem. The teftimony of Dr. Waterland muft be confidered as no vulgar
voucher. To coincide with one, who feems
to have left no recefs of Ecclefiaftical Antiquity unexplored, and who never failed to
apply with accuracy the refult of his profound inveftigations to the vindication of the
Catholic Faith, cannot but infpire great and
well-grounded confidence in any caufe, involved in the opinion of the primitive Church.
Dr. Waterland then concludes an examination of fome paffages of Juftin Martyr, the
moft confiderable of thofe writers who are
fometimes fufpected of favouring a temporal
Generation, with the following fentence.
" Thefe confiderations convince me that Juf-
" tin, as well as Athenagoras, taught the
" ftrict Co-eternity of the Son; which is
" equally true of all the other writers '.
The moft compendious, and at the fame
time, the faireft, mode of demonftrating the
wide difference between Mr. Hawtrey and

* Firft Defence of his Queries, p. 155.

thofe

thofe Fathers who on a curfory view may be thought to favour him, will be to contraſt with his hypotheſis the moſt favourable paſſage of the moſt favourable writer. That writer, I believe, is Hippolytus; and that paſſage, as follows [t]. " Qualem igitur filium " fuum Deus per carnem miſit, niſi verbum, " quod a principio ſcilicet filium vocavit, " quia futurum erat ut ortum caperet? et " cum filius vocatur, commune nomen amo-" ris erga homines fumit. Nec enim Ver-" bum per ſe et *fine carne* perfeƌtus filius " erat, cum tamen eſſet perfectum verbum, " unigenitus." This paſſage, taken in an unqualified ſenſe, is glaringly inconſiſtent with many others; it is inconſiſtent with the one already quoted; with that in which he af-firms the Word to have become Son, when God ſaid, Let there be light; and indeed with the general tenour of his ſtyle in the 16th chapter, in which he comments on the Verbi *generatio*. But as his words are *perfeƌtus* Filius, there is a fort of gradation implied, from which we may conclude that he annexed *fome* notion of Filiation to his prior ſtate of Exiſtence; and may be thus made conſiſtent with himſelf.

[t] S. Hippolyti contra Noetum, c. xv. p. 242. Ed. Fab.

But

But further; the phraſeology of the Fathers ſupplies us with an argument in proof of their belief in the *Son*'s co-eternity, which will extend, almoſt indiſcriminately, to all. Though the fact on which it is grounded ſeems to be doubted by Mr. Hawtrey, I ſhall at preſent aſſume it, as it will be neceſſary to prove it hereafter. All the Fathers apply to the λόγος ſuch epithets as μονοʃενὴς and πρωτότοκος. Now as the terms only-begotten and generation; and the terms firſt-born and filiation reciprocally imply each other; as where there is a firſt-born, there muſt have been a filiation, or where there is an only-begotten, there muſt have been a generation; they who explicitly maintained the one, implicitly maintained the other. Upon the whole; whatever ſhades of difference may be diſcerned in the language in which they ſpeak of the Son's eternal exiſtence, his proceſſion and his nativity, there is no diſcordance on the main point; if they thought his Incarnation *a* Filiation, as it undoubtedly was, they did not think it the only one; and if they called his coming forth to create the world *a* Generation, yet by their application of only-begotten and firſtborn to the λόγος, they muſt have thought that

that that Generation had been preceded by another ".

Thus, then, do we find the Fathers of the three firſt centuries aſſerting in language too conſiſtent to have been dictated by errour, and too frequent to have ariſen from chance, the Eternal Filiation of the Son of God. As they by their unanimity afford to each other mutual confirmation and mutual credit ; ſo too, will much of that veneration, with which we are wont to receive the Decrees of the Nicene Council, be withdrawn, if we find them innovating on any doctrine, thus ſanctified by the voice of Antiquity, and the moſt perfect harmony of the Fathers.

Before we proceed to examine the Nicene Creed, it will not be foreign to our ſubject to obſerve, that in the Greek Formula of renouncing the Jewiſh Religion, as given us by Cotelerius ˣ, we find a profeſſion of belief in the only-begotten Son and Word of God, τῦ ἐκ Πατρὸς πρὸ πάντων τῶν αἰώνων γεννηθέντος. The Council of Antioch too, which was aſſembled fifty nine-years before that of Nice, in its Profeſſio Fidei, uſes theſe plain and de-

---

" Sed quoniam præclaram præter omnes habuit in ſe eam quæ eſt ab altiſſimo Patre genituram, præclara autem functus eſt et eâ, quæ eſt ex Virgine, Generatione. Iren. l. iii. c. 21. p. 249.
ˣ Patres Apoſt. tom. i. p. 505.

ciſive

cifive words ; "[y] Hunc autem Filium geni-
" tum, unigenitum, imaginem Dei invifibi-
" lis, primogenitum omnis creaturæ, fapien-
" tiam, et verbum ac virtutem, Dei *ante fæ-*
" *cula,* non præcognitione, fed fubftantia et
" hypoftafi Deum, Dei Filium, cum in ve-
" teri et novo Teftamento cognoverimus,
" confitemur et prædicamus."

A little attention to the origin of the
Council of Nice will give us correcter views
of the object, which the Emperor propofed
to himfelf in convoking it, and a clearer in-
fight into its final decifions. In the Ecclefiaftical hiftory of that age we find recorded
a difpute between Alexander, Bifhop of Alexandria, and Arius, the founder of the fect,
fince diftinguifhed by his name, on a queftion, in the fate of which was involved the
Eternal Generation of the Son of God. For
Arius is there reprefented arguing, that if
the Father begot the Son, the Son muft
have had a *beginning* of his exiftence, and
thence deducing, as a manifeft confequence,
that there was a time when the Son was
not [z]. The Bifhop, fhocked at fuch an Anti-

---

[y] Concil. omnium General. tom. i. p. 545.

[z] Φησὶν (fcil. Arius) εἰ ὁ Πατὴρ ἐγέννησε τὸν υἱὸν, ἀρχὴν ὑπάρξεως ἔχει ὁ γεννηθείς· κᾳ ἐκ τούτυ δῆλον, ὅτι ἦν ὅτε ἀκ ἦν ὁ υἱός. Socrat.
l. i. c. 5. p. 9. Ed. Reading. Sozom. l. i. c. 15. p. 31. and
Theodorit.

christian doctrine, refutes it by scriptural proofs, introduced into the circular letter [a], in which he pronounces an Anathema on the propagators of the Arian tenets. Arius, however, had his supporters, for a fancied object of persecution will never want them; and with this religious discussion was soon associated an intolerant spirit of party, which Constantine by the mild exercise of his authority in vain endeavoured to subdue. Unable therefore by the influence of exhortation to compose the difference, he invited the Bishops from every part of Christendom to assemble at Nice, in order to debate and determine the question [b]. Would it not then be matter of just astonishment, if in the creed of this celebrated Council we should find no clue to guide us to their important decision on the subject? Would there not be something incredibly perverse in their conduct, if they transmitted to posterity their sentiments on all other articles of faith, for the ascertaining the truth of which they were not convened, and yet withheld their opinion on the very subject for the full and final discussion of which they were ex-

Theodorit. c. ii. p. 7; where the Historian distinguishes Alexander, by the emphatic title, ἀποστολικῶν δογμάτων συνήγορος.

[a] Socrat. c. vi.   [b] c. vii.

presly

prefsly affembled ? A doubt, I am aware, about the pafchal feaft operated as an additional motive for convening the Council; but that can only be confidered as a fubordinate one; or whatever be thought of its relative importance, as they actually did come to a determination on that point, the prefumption is ftill ftronger that they would treat the other with equal refpect. If, as Socrates informs us, Chriftianity, from the diffenfions which this controverfy had engendered, was an object of public and theatrical derifion *before* [c], the circumftance of a Chriftian Synod, fo renowned for its numbers, its dignity, and its talents, meeting for the exprefs purpofe of regiftering their faith on a fpecific article, and feparating without effectuating that purpofe, could not but increafe and perpetuate the derifion. This then is a ftrong a priori argument for there having originally been in the creed fome declaration of their belief in the Eternal Generation; for as we know that Arius was exiled and his doctrine profcribed, their declaration muft unavoidably run counter to his tenets, and ftrike at the very root of his herefy. But here arifes a difficulty, of no gigantic fize

---

[c] Ὅτι δημοσίᾳ καὶ ἐν αὐτοῖς θεάτροις τὸν Χριστιανισμὸν γελᾶσθαι. c. vi.

however,

however, out of an opinion which Mr. Hawtrey has ftarted, that " the doctrine of the
" Eternal Generation ftrongly favours the
" caufe of Arianifm [d]." To me the opinion
feems not for a moment maintainable. Unlefs the creed of Arius is a rhapfody of para-
doxes, (and I feel no inclination to refcue it
from fuch a charge, though its general boaft
is, that it is confiftent with the deductions
of reafon) the Eternal Generation could not
poffibly be maintained by him, whofe conftant pofition was, ἦν ὅτε ἐκ ἦν ὁ ΥΙΟΣ. If
this be doubted, as Arius cannot be denied
to be a fair interpreter of his own doctrines,
let us refer to his Letters to Alexander Bifhop
of Alexandria, and Eufebius Bifhop of Nicomedia ; in which he fortunately furnifhes us
with the means of determining what his heterodoxy confifted in, by explaining both his
own opinion, and the oppofite one of his
Perfecutor, Alexander. In the firft of thefe
Letters, in which he makes an oftentatious
enumeration of feveral articles relating to the
Son, in which he profeffes to believe, and in
which he affects to have been inftructed by
the Bifhop himfelf, we ftill find him deny-
ing his *Eternity* [e]. This fimilarity of fenti-

[d] Θεάνθρωπος, p. 185.
[e] Οὐδὶ γὰρ ἐςιν ἀίδιος, ἢ συναίδιος. Epiph. l. ii. tom. ii. p.
733. Ed. Petav.

F   ment

ment which he would here infinuate, by re-
ferring the origin of his creed to the Bifhop,
is not to be reconciled with that broad difference which his own ftatement here and
elfewhere authorizes us to fay exifted between them. In his Letter to Eufebius, he
himfelf profeffes to believe that " the Son
" in will and défign exifted before all time,
" but yet that he had a *beginning* ;" and declares that it was the affertion of that *commencement* of the Son's exiftence, which was
the caufe of his perfecution [f]. Aware of the
congenial reception which his herefy would
meet with from the Bifhop of Nicomedia ;
to him, we fee, he is more difpofed to un-
bofom his mind. But that he really and
truly believed all which he there profeffes,
the extended amount of which certainly falls
fhort of a belief in the Eternal Generation,
may reafonably be doubted ; as Epiphanius
affures us that he modified his own heretical
tenets by an hypocritical affectation of orthodox terms ; προσεποιεῖτο εἰρωνείᾳ τὰ τῆς ὀρ-
θοδοξίας ῥήματα [g]. Let us give him, however,
the credit of fincerity ; and even then he
differs moft effentially from his adverfary ;

[f] Θελήματι καὶ βολῇ ὑπέστη πρὸ χρόνων καὶ πρὸ αἰώνων——πρὶν γεν-
νηθῇ, ἐκ ἦν. And again ; διωτόμεθα ὅτι εἴπαμεν, ΑΡΧΗΝ ἔχει ὁ
υἱός. Theodorit. c. v. p. 22. Ed. Reading.

[g] Epiph. l. ii. tom. ii. p. 720.

for *be* maintained that there was no iota of time conceivable fo fmall as to intervene between the exiftence of God and the exiftence of the Son [h]. In conformity with thefe tenets which Arius imputes to him, Alexander, in his Letter to the Bifhop of Conftantinople, fays that " he haftened to expofe their " *infidelity*, who fay, that there was a time " when the *Son* was *not* [l]." If then we have fucceeded in fhewing that the Eternal Generation was maintained by Alexander and denied by Arius, the opinion of its favouring the caufe of Arianifm muft in candour be abandoned ; with Grabe we may fay, the Eternity of the *Son* is " e diametro Ariano- " rum hærefi adverfa [k] ;" and every trace of that prejudice, which the avowal of fuch opinion was intended to create againft the doctrine, muft be obliterated in the mind. For the reafon, adduced by Mr. Hawtrey, as demonftrative of that fupport which Arianifm is to derive from the doctrine of the Eternal Generation, is alike vulnerable. " If " the doctrine is true," fays he [l], " then " Chrift was always, *as being a Son*, fubordi-

[h] Ἀεὶ ὁ Θεὸς, ἀεὶ ὁ Υἱός· συνυπάρχει ἀγεννήτως ὁ Τιὸς τῷ Θεῷ· —— ὅτι ἐπινοίᾳ, ὅτι ἀτόμῳ τινὶ προάγει ὁ Θεὸς τῦ Υἱῦ. Theodorit. c. v. p. 22. ut fupra. [i] Theodorit. c. iv. p. 11.
[k] Not. in Iren. p. 138. [l] Θεάνθρωπος, p. 185.

" nate

" nate and inferior to the Father; then was
" he always alſo, as having the Divine Na-
" ture by neceſſity, an inferior ſubordinate
" God, which, I apprehend, was the doc-
" trine of Arius." What the doctrine of
Arius with reſpect to the Son was, we have
already ſeen; and though the doctrine of the
Catholic Church certainly is that the Son in
his pre-exiſting ſtate is ſubordinate to the Father; yet it is a ſubordination, which totally
excludes inferiority; it is a ſubordination of
order, not an inferiority of Nature; and he,
who has not firſt expoſed the fallacy of Dr.
Waterland's accurate diſtinction, in his Defence of his Queries ᵐ, can have no right to
confound inferior with ſubordinate, or to
paſs with inadvertent rapidity from an acknowledgment of the one to an aſſertion of
the other.

If Mr. Hawtrey ſhould ſtill impute to
thoſe, who maintain the Eternal Generation,
an affection for Arianiſm, we may fairly re-
taliate the imputation of heterodoxy, and re-
mind him of that hæreſiarch, Servetus, who,
according to Father Paul ⁿ, eſpouſed the opi-

ᵐ Waterland's Defence of his Queries, p. 71. 183. 300.
302. 447.
ⁿ " Defenſeur de l'ancienne opinion de Paul de Samoſate."
Hiſtoire du Concile de Trente, tom. ii. p. 14. à Londres.

nion

nion of Paul of Samofata, which opinion,
we have already feen, the Council of Antioch
condemned in a decree which afferts the
Eternal Generation; and who, according to
Beza, " Chriftum contendebat *humanæ dun-*
" *taxat naturæ* refpectu *Filium* Dei dici, id-
" eoque *æternum Filium* effe negabat °."

To refume, then, our argument. The
leading object, for which the Synod was
convened, makes the original infertion of
fome claufe or other in the Creed relating
to the Filiation extremely probable; and the
fact of Arius's banifhment, who denied the
Eternal Generation, makes it almoft certain
that fuch claufe would affert it. And in
truth we have the authority of the Epiftle
which the Council circulated, for contending
that they did actually anathematize Arius for
this very dogma ᵖ; as well as that of Sozo-
men for afferting, both that they themfelves
maintained the Co-eternity of the Son with
the Father ᑫ, and excommunicated thofe who
oppofed it ʳ. This train of reafoning then
may perhaps be allowed to corroborate the

° Beza in Epift. Pauli ad Coloff. c. i. 15.
ᵖ Παμψηφεὶ ἔδοξεν ἀναθεματισθῆναι τὴν ἀσεβῆ αὐτῦ δόξαν—εἶναι
ποτὶ ὅτι ἐκ ἦν. Socrat. Hift. Ecclef. c. ix. p. 26.
ᑫ Συνίγραται δὲ Ἄρμος μὲν τοῖς παρ' αὐτῦ εἰρημένοις· ΟΙ ΔΕ, ὡς ὁμο-
ύσιος καὶ ΣΥΝΑΙΔΙΟΣ ἐστιν Ὁ ΥΙΟΣ τῷ Πατρί. c. xv. p. 32.
ʳ Τὰς λέγοντας ἦν ποτὶ ὅτι ἐκ ἦν—ἀπεκήρυξαν. c. xxi. p. 39.

opinion,

opinion, that this controverted Claufe, if not adopted by the Nicene Fathers whilft the Council was fitting, was however inferted by them immediately after its diffolution.

But what are we to fay to Mr. Hawtrey's inuendo [a], that it was introduced by Eufebius, who was fufpected, whether juftly or not he does not determine, of favouring the Arian caufe. Mofheim and his Annotator think the fufpicion groundlefs [t] ; but be that as it may. Let us fuppofe for a moment that this difputed claufe is not repugnant to Arianifm ; and even, to ufe Mr. Hawtrey's own words [u], that we are indebted for it to the indefatigable induftry of the Arians. And indefatigable indeed they muft have been in their induftry, as well as daring in their innovation. For Mr. Hawtrey allows that it was in the creed, prior to the fecond General Council ; fo that really one does not know which to admire moft ; the confummate effrontery of the Arians, who could fo foon think of foifting one of their heretical tenets into a creed which proclaimed them heretics, or the accommodating inactivity of the orthodox who tamely fuffered it. As for

[a] Θεάνθρωπος, p. 183.
[t] Ecclef. Hiftory, vol. i. p. 187. Ed. 4to.
[u] Θεάνθρωπος, p. 186.

the

the audacity of the Arians, I can readily admit it ; though ftratagem, I think, was their characteriftic rather than boldnefs : but furely amidft the illuftrious advocates of Chriftianity, and there were many of them in thofe times of religious conflict, there would have been fome who would not have been fo blind as not to fee, nor fo fupine as not to expofe, the forgery. Nay, fo palpable muft it have been, on the idea, I mean, that it was coined in the Arian mint, that even a common obferver, however unaccuftomed to the fubtleties of diftinction or unexercifed in the arts of reafoning, could not have caft a glance into the Creed without exclaiming, " non " erat his locus."

But Baronius, it feems, afferts that the Acts of the Nicene Council had been loft partly by the efforts of the Arians[x]. There are thofe who think that Baronius was miftaken, in fuppofing that the Acts of the Council were ever committed to writing[y] : but even if they were, and taking the paffage quoted by Mr. Hawtrey in its moft comprehenfive fenfe, Baronius does not fay

---

[x] Θεάνθρωπος, p. 186.
[y] Baronium decepit Latina interpretatio Athanafii in lib. de Synod. &c.—Critica in Annal. Baron. fec. iv. p. 90. auctore Anton. Pagi.

a fyllable

a fyllable of their having tampered with the Creed. And in fact, a few pages after this paffage, on the ftrength of which Mr. Haw-trey afcribes to the claufe in difpute an Arian extraction, Baronius informs us why, the Council inferted the additional word ὁμο-ὑσιον [z]. If we had not already proved, Baronius certainly would for us, that the Council afferted a Generation abfolutely eternal, and that the Arians denied any fuch thing except in *will* and *defign*, Θελήματι καὶ βυλῇ. Under this reftriction, (and by the help of a little mental refervation they could underftand it when it was not expreffed) they would not have hefitated to fubfcribe to the claufe. The Nicene Fathers therefore, aware of their equivocating arts, added ὁμοὑσιον as being free from all ambiguity, and fecured againft all evafion. But, although they refifted the claufe, till fortified with ὁμοὑσιον, becaufe it did not affert the *Co-eternity* with fufficient clearnefs, yet having by their declaration of the Confubftantiality of the Son with the

---

[z] Plane *imperfecta* effe oftendatur et informis, quæ nec Arii *excludebat* impietatem, et nihil penitus habebat de co-æquali-tate, *co-æternitate*, et effentia Filii cum ipfo Patre ; ac proinde ejufmodi effe, quâ Arius uti *poffet*, et Ariani. Quamobrem ad eludendam (ut dictum eft) vafriciem et fubdolum confilium Ariani hominis, Confubftantiale Verbum Patri jure meritoque patres *addendum* putarunt. Baron. Annal. Eccl. tom. ii. p. 393.

Father

Father once provided againſt the Arian ſubterfuge (and for which Mr. Hawtrey [a] ſeems
to have a little affection) they could have no
longer any difficulty in admitting it [b]; becauſe, though it was capable of being dif-
torted by Arian duplicity, unleſs aſſent alſo
was given to the Son's Conſubſtantiality, yet
when coupled with ſuch aſſent it could not
be deemed liable to any tergiverſation whatever.   Upon the whole then, as far as Baronius can be made to prove any thing, the
Council of Nice were ſo far from not ſanc-
tioning the doctrine of the Eternal Generation, or, as Mr. Hawtrey ſays [c], from expunging the clauſe which aſſerted it, that
they only pauſed about the inſertion of it
from an apprehenſion that it might not be
worded in a manner ſufficiently poſitive and
clear.   That it was from theſe conſiderations
that Archbiſhop Uſher adopted his opinion,
it might be thought preſumption to ſuppoſe;
but yet, this view of the ſubject certainly
points to the ſame concluſion.   " Nicænos
" Patres primæ Symboli parti ab Euſebio ex

---

[a] Preface to Θεάνθρωπος, p. 13.
[b] " The Arians (ſays Dr. Cave) repreſented their propoſi-
" tions in ſuch general terms, and were ſo ſubtile and deceitful
" in their explications, that the Fathers thought they could
" never particularly enough provide againſt them." Apoſtolici,
p. 362.   [c] Θεάνθρωπος, p. 183.

" vetere

" vetere formula primùm propofitæ, et ab
" eis plenius explicatæ, alteram deinde quæ
" fupererat partem adjunxiffe: vel eorum po-
" tiùs primarios aliquos, poft folutum Conci-
" lium, id effeciffe [d]."

But to whatever clafs of readings this difputed claufe be affigned; our caufe, even if
it were to be decided by the general tenour
of the Nicene Creed, is by no means a defpe-
rate one. In that Creed, in the ftate in
which Mr. Hawtrey imagines it to have
come from the hands of the Fathers themfelves, uninjured by time and unmutilated
by Arianifm, there are expreffions applied to
the Son, which could not poffibly, I think,
be applied to him by thofe, who did not believe in his eternal exiftence *as Son*. In the
firft place, he is faid to be ὁμοούσιος; and he
furely, who is confubftantial with the Father,
muft of courfe have all his effential proper-
ties, of which Eternity is one. This argument is fo ably purfued by Mr. Stephens in
his Sermon, before quoted, where he fhews
that the Fathers, by afferting the Son to
have been begotten of the fubftance of the
Father, affert the Eternal Generation [e], that

---

[d] De Symb. p. 9. Append. ad Ufferii Annales.
[e] So too Waterland, p. 266. of his fecond Defence. " I
" might add further proofs, from Juftin, of the Son's neceffary
" exiftence; the fame that Bifhop Bull has produced out of
                                                    " him

I have only to remark that the fame reafoning will of courfe apply to the fame language ufed by the Nicene Council; and to add this ftronger circumftance in juftification of the fenfe we attach to the word, that Baronius informs us the Council purpofely adopted it in order to record their belief of his Co-eternity. Should the folidity of this reafoning be attempted to be fhaken, by faying, that as the Son was a Being compounded of two natures, of which the λόγος was an eternal one and manhood an affumed one, therefore Confubftantiality is afcribed to him from his union with the former; it is a mere fophifm, which a diftinct view of Mr. Hawtrey's own hypothefis will be fufficient to refute. For as he fuppofes the Filiation to confift in an union of the λόγος with human Nature; it is evident that before that union he could not be Son, and of courfe, quatenus Son, could not be eternal, and therefore not confubftantial. For Confubftantiality with God cannot poffibly originate in a participation of mortality, but muft be eternal as the Fons Deitatis from which it flowed. Of no finite being then can this Confubftantiality be predicated; of no one, as fuch, in

" him for the Confubftantiality; *for whatever proves one, proves* " *both.*"

any

any relative capacity, for the commencement of which any period within the limits
of time can be affigned : but, whoever that
Subject or Perfon be, in whom Confubftantiality with God is inherent, muft of neceffity be eternal. That Perfon, according to
the Nicene Fathers, is the Son ; fo that unlefs we withhold from them the credit of
knowing what words were proper vehicles
of their own ideas, they meant to affert,
what in point of fact they do affert, the
eternal exiftence of the Son. But further ;
the Creed fets forth that by him (the Son)
" were all things made." Now it is clear, I
fhould imagine, that the Framers of the
Creed would not have attributed to him, in
the capacity of the Son of God, any agency
before the creation of the world, if they
had meant to *difown* a prior Filiation. More-
over the Creed declares that he (the Son)
" came down from Heaven, and was incar-
" nate" &c. If then St. John's expreffion
that " the *Word* was made flefh " is to be
conftrued into an implied affertion, that he
was only Word and not Son before that period, this expreffion of the Nicene Fathers
that the *Son* was incarnate muft equally
prove that they believed him to be *Son before*
he was made flefh. I do not mean to ba-
lance

lance one authority againſt the other ; but I
cannot but maintain that upon the ſame
principle of interpretation on which St.
John's language is made to prove that the
Filiation conſiſted *in* the Incarnation, the
language of the Nicene Council proves that
it had taken place *before*. Laſtly, the ex-
communicating clauſe, annexed to the Creed,
ſhews that they meant to proſcribe the doctrine of a Filiation which was not eternal.
Τὲς δὲ λέγοντας, ἥν ποτὲ ὅτε ἐκ ἦν, ἥ ἐκ ἦν πρὶν
γεννηθῆναι —— ἥ τρεπτὸν, ἥ ἀλλοιωτὸν τὸν υἱὸν τοῦ
Θεῦ, τύτες ἀναθεματίζει ἡ καθολικὴ καὶ ἀποςο-
λακὴ τῦ Θεῦ Ἐκκλησία.

As the Doctrine of Athanaſius is exploded
by Mr. Hawtrey, I muſt of courſe wave
every appeal, in corroboration of what has
been ſaid, to him. But yet, I muſt obſerve,
what indeed will occur to every one who
reads the Hiſtory of the Nicene Council,
that the active and diſtinguiſhed part, which
Athanaſius took in it, would hardly have
been tolerated, nay would have called down
rebukes from the Emperor and the Biſhops,
if his Doctrine had not been deemed the
Doctrine of Scripture. Inſtead of this, it
muſt be remembered, he was ſoon after re-
warded with the See of Alexandria.

Thus then with regard to the Council of
Nice,

Nice, it should seem that if they paused about the admission of the suspected clause, it was only till they had guarded against the trickeries of Arian interpretation; or that even if they rejected the clause, they did not reject the doctrine; and therefore to deny the Eternal Filiation *would* be in us " a de-" parture from the Nicene Faith [f]."

There remains to be examined only one other topic, which, though not decked out in all the formalities of argument, is, I fancy, intended to operate as such. Eusebius, when he styles our Lord πρωτόγονος λόγος is accused of holding language, unprecedented and unauthorized [g]: and yet a critic [h], who was ἐχ ὁ τύχων ἄνηρ, calls him " virum in re " *veteri* Christianorum versatissimum." If however this application of the word be really unsupported by the example of the Fathers; it ought certainly to be received with suspicion and distrust; and might perhaps, in defect of positive evidence to the contrary, be considered as a proof that, in their minds, any term expressive of Generation could not be predicated of the λόγος.

[f] Θεάνθρωπος, p. 182.
[g] " Which, I suppose, was never used by any one, prior to " himself," &c. Θεάνθρωπος, p. 182.
[h] Wesseling. Probab. c. i. p. 5.

But

But this furmife of Eufebius being an innovator on the eftablifhed appropriation of the epithet πρωτόγονος may be eafily fhewn to be groundlefs. It is not for the fake merely of vindicating Eufebius that I will endeavour concifely to oppofe to Mr. Hawtrey, the flat contradiction of the Fathers; but becaufe this vindication will fhew, that, by the language which they ufed, they muft have affociated the idea of Filiation with λόγος.

Thus Juftin Martyr [1] calls the λόγος ΠΡΩΤΟΝ ΓΕΝΝΗΜΑ τῦ Θεῦ in one place, and in others πρωτότοκος τῷ Θεῷ. Theophilus [k], we have already feen, applies ἐγέννησε, γεννήσας, and πρωτότοκος to the λόγος. Irenæus [l] ufes the expreffion " unigenitum Dei Verbum." Tatian [m] fays of the λόγος, both that he was ἔργον πρωτότοκον, and ἐν ἀρχῇ γεννηθείς. Hippolytus [n] in one paffage has " generabat Ver-" bum," in another λόγος μονογενής, in another λόγος πρὸ πάντων γεγεννημένος, and in another λογῦ γένεσις. Tertullian [o] defines λόγον, " Verbum illud primordiale, primogenitum;"

---

[1] Apol. Prim. p. 31. 54. 94. Ed. Thirlby.
[k] Ad Autol. l. ii. p. 81. 129.
[l] Iren. l. ii. c. 49. p. 177. Ed. Grabe.
[m] p. 21, 22. Ed. Worth.
[n] Contra Noetum, p. 13. 17, 18. et de Anti-Chrift. p. 14. Ed. Fabric.
[o] Adverfus Prax. c. vii. p. 504.

and

and fays, " quæcunque fubftantia Sermonis
" fuit, illam dico perfonam, et illi nomen
" *Filii* vindico." In Origen, [p] we find λογῦ
μονογενῦς, and in Theodotus, [q] πρωτοκτιςὸν λόγον.

More examples of the fame phrafeology
might be adduced ; but thefe probably are
enough to anfwer the double purpofe for
which they are intended ; and he who re-
flects on the ideas conveyed in the epithets
here applied to the λόγος, may perhaps bold-
ly afk with St. Chryfoftom, φιλονεικήσας τῷ
μονογενεῖ τῆς υἰότητος [r];

In conclufion ; I would fhortly notice the
yerfe in the firft Epiftle to the Corinthians,
which gave birth to Mr. Hawtrey's hypothefis, " Then fhall the Son alfo himfelf be
" fubject unto him, that put all things under
" him, that God may be all in all [s]." And here
I would obferve, that as the confideration of
the twofold nature of our bleffed Lord re-
conciles many feeming contradictions of fcriptural language, fo too, in our endeavour to
explain the Apoftle's meaning, may we derive the fame advantages from the confidera-

---

[p] Athanaf. Epift. de Decret. p. 233. tom. 1. Ed. par.
[q] Fabric. Bib. Græc. tom. v. Ed. Par.
[r] Chryfoft. in cap. i. Johan. p. 22. Ed. Fronto Ducæ.
[s] c. xv. ver. 28.

tion

Check Out More Titles From HardPress Classics Series In this collection we are offering thousands of classic and hard to find books. This series spans a vast array of subjects – so you are bound to find something of interest to enjoy reading and learning about.

Subjects:
Architecture
Art
Biography & Autobiography
Body, Mind &Spirit
Children & Young Adult
Dramas
Education
Fiction
History
Language Arts & Disciplines
Law
Literary Collections
Music
Poetry
Psychology
Science
…and many more.

Visit us at www.hardpress.net

CPSIA information can be obtained
at www.ICGtesting.com
Printed in the USA
BVHW082003260819
556819BV00017B/4459/P